The Art and Science
of Business Valuation

The Art and Science of Business Valuation

Albert N. Link and Michael B. Boger

Foreword by James H. Ogburn

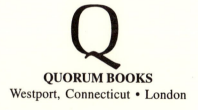

QUORUM BOOKS
Westport, Connecticut • London

Library of Congress Cataloging-in-Publication Data

Link, Albert N.
    The art and science of business valuation / Albert N. Link and
    Michael B. Boger ; foreword by James H. Ogburn.
        p.   cm.
    Includes bibliographical references and index.
    ISBN 1–56720–171–7 (alk. paper)
    1. Business enterprises—Valuation.   I. Boger, Michael B.
    II. Title.
    HG4028.V3L555   1999
    658.15—dc21   99–10383

British Library Cataloguing in Publication Data is available.

Library of Congress Catalog Card Number: 99–10383
ISBN: 1–56720–171–7

First published in 1999

Quorum Books, 88 Post Road West, Westport, CT 06881
An imprint of Greenwood Publishing Group, Inc.
www.quorumbooks.com

Printed in the United States of America

The paper used in this book complies with the
Permanent Paper Standard issued by the National
Information Standards Organization (Z39.48–1984).

10 9 8 7 6 5 4 3 2 1

For our families

CONTENTS

TABLES AND FIGURES

TABLES

FIGURES

FOREWORD

There has been an explosion in the valuation profession during the 1990s. Not only has there been a dramatic increase in the number of valuations being conducted, but there also has been an associated increase in the number of would-be valuators. *The Art and Science of Business Valuation* will serve the latter community well.

While there are many texts and professional reference guides available, most tend to present only the "science" of valuation and leave the reader to conclude that a business valuation is little more than a matter-of-fact exercise. Obviously, this is not the case. From my experience, it is unproductive to introduce practitioner students—and we are all students from time to time when it comes to our professional acquisition of new skills and ideas—to new concepts by exposing them only to formalistic approaches. What practitioner students need is intuitive insight into the topic, and the topic's application limitations, along with the tools that are relevant to the topic (in addition to their strengths and limitations). Albert N. Link and Michael B. Boger have provided the growing valuation profession with just such a primer.

The Art and Science of Business Valuation is a clearly written and brilliantly presented introductory overview of business valuation methods. The authors are forthright in their presentation of this subject, honestly emphasizing what is art and what is science. I believe that all readers will find the Link and Boger approach refreshing and highly informative.

James H. Ogburn
President, Accounting Education Associates, Inc.

PREFACE

Business valuation is a pervasive activity that, in our opinion, is truly understood by only a few of those involved in the science of its practice. Those who do understand the concepts and methods of business valuation are aware that business valuation is both an art as well as a science. In response to the rapidly growing involvement of professionals in this area, we set forth in this book basic fundamental principles.

This is an introductory book or primer. Certainly there is a surfeit of technical manuals on the topic of business valuation, many of which are published by professional associations as part of continuing education for their members. This book does not fit that genre. Rather, our emphasis is less on the mechanical science of business valuation and more on the intuitive art of business valuation, with emphasis on the distinction between the two. Based on over three decades of experience in conducting business valuations and teaching the associated methodologies, we have matured to conclude that the most useful information a novice valuator can possess is an understanding that there are elements of art and science in the practice of business valuation and an appreciation that both elements are important.

Our sincere appreciation goes to many individuals who have been supportive throughout the preparation of this book. First and foremost are our families. Our wonderful wives, especially, through their patience, have shown support for this project. Second, Jim Sabin of Greenwood Publishing Group has been enthusiastic about this project from its inception, and this enthusiasm and his expert editorial guidance are reflected herein. Third, many individuals have favored us by reading early manuscript drafts and offering their learned comments and suggestions. We especially note Scott Gayle, John Morrow, and Carolyn Woodruff. To all of these people, our sincere thanks.

1

INTRODUCTION

All I know is what I read in the papers.
—Will Rogers

This is an introductory book on business valuation. By introductory we mean that the material presented in these chapters provides the novice business valuator with an overview of business valuation concepts and techniques related in large part to closely held businesses. By novice business valuator we mean an individual who wishes to understand the basic concepts of business valuation, the assumptions that underlie those concepts, and the appropriate ways to apply those concepts. Our purpose in this book is not to educate the "experienced" business valuator about new statistical methods or valuation interpretations, but rather to lay a foundation for those new or relatively new to the field.

It is our opinion, however, that the value of the experience of many so-called "expert" valuators may be somewhat in the eyes of the beholder. It is not always the case that the individual who has conducted the greatest number of business valuations is necessarily the most experienced valuator. It could very well be the case that such an involved individual has done little more than implement (correctly or incorrectly) one valuation method and then replicate it hundreds of times. Our intention in making such a blunt statement is that experience in the field of business valuation comes not from repetition of the application of methods but rather from repeated thought about the intent of the methods. The truly experienced business valuator is the one who, paraphrasing Will Rogers, has done more than just read about business valuations. The truly experienced business valuator can, for example, explain why a particular concept of value was initially selected or why a particular method of application of the selected concept of value was employed. More importantly, the truly experienced business valuator can explain why unused concepts and methods are less appropriate for the particular valuation under question. This level of insight includes more than just the ability to explain what numbers were put into what formulae.

Thus, we approach business valuation with a strong emphasis on the assumptions that underlie valuation methods rather than on the mechanics.

We expect that one of three types of individuals will find this book useful and have written it accordingly. These three types of individuals fall roughly into the following categories, which, of course, are not mutually exclusive:

- individuals who are contemplating buying or selling a business,
- attorneys with cases involving business valuations, and
- accountants who are seeking an overview of business valuation methods and practices.

There are many reasons why such individuals, and many others, would seek a general understanding of the subtleties of conducting a business valuation. It would be ideal in this introductory chapter to emphasize our point in a quantitative manner, but to do so would require data on the number of valuations conducted each year and the myriad reasons for conducting the valuations. Unfortunately, to our knowledge, no such information exists, and if it did we expect the number of valuations conducted each year would be in the millions, having increased over time, and the purposes for such valuations would number in the thousands.

Instead, we emphasize the breadth of interest in an understanding of the elements of business valuation by listing five general areas in which business valuations are important, and for which, based on our experience, they are undertaken. This list is not inclusive but illustrative given the interests and background of our expected audience. These areas are:

- mergers and acquisitions,
- buy/sell agreements,
- acquisitions of capital,
- estate planning, and
- litigation support.

MERGERS AND ACQUISITIONS

In the most general sense, the terms merger and acquisition refer to the exchange of ownership control of a business enterprise. Company A and Company B may merge and form a new composite company; Company A may purchase or acquire Company B, or vice versa. In either situation, it is imperative that both companies—and there could be more than two companies—be valued either formally or informally.

For illustrative purposes, assume that Company A seeks to acquire Company B. Then, Company A will need to know the value of Company B before establishing a purchase price. Company B will need to approximate its own value before beginning to negotiate with Company A. Because Company A has a financial incentive to offer to pay Company B as low a price as possible, and because Company B has a similar incentive to ask Company A for as high a price as possible, it is to be expected that both companies' initial valuations will differ and by a large amount. Owing to such asymmetry in terms of the underlying financial incentives, it is fundamentally important for both parties to understand the principles of business valuation so as to anticipate and, more importantly, to interpret the other's offer.

Table 1.1 shows the number of public mergers and acquisitions initiated in the United States in 1990 and in 1996, the most recent year for which these data are available. The number of mergers and acquisitions increased 33 percent over this six-year time interval, and the value of the mergers and acquisitions increased 415 percent. Regarding the 5,639 mergers and acquisitions recorded in 1996, at a minimum 11,278 valuations were conducted—one by each party—and many more were undertaken for which data were not publicly available.

Table 1.1
Merger and Acquisition Activity in the United States

	1990	1996
Number of mergers and acquisitions	4,239	5,639
Value of mergers and acquisitions	$205.6 billion	$1,059.3 billion

Note: Includes public transactions valued at $5 million or more.

Source: U.S. Department of Commerce, *Statistical Abstract of the United States, 1998*, p. 556.

BUY/SELL AGREEMENTS

Owners of closely held businesses always want to control the dispersion of the ownership interests of their businesses. For this reason, contractual agreements are often made restricting the transfer of ownership of the business—buying or selling—as well as establishing methodologies for valuing those ownership interests. These contractual agreements are called buy/sell agreements.

Whether the business is a formal partnership or corporation, situations frequently arise where one owner will need to sell his or her ownership interest. Sales of ownership interests are common not only in goods-producing businesses but also in service-producing businesses, such as medical or legal practices. A buy/sell agreement sets forth the terms for all future purchases and sales of ownership of the business.

The contractual formula in buy/sell agreements for determining ownership value often appears to be very simple. The formula, at least in principle, is tied to more complex formulas used in formal business valuations. However, when buy/sell agreements are initially developed or revised, formal valuations are generally conducted to assure the owners that the contractually agreed-upon formula accurately reflects the value of the business.

In 1995, the most recent data available, there were approximately 1.6 million partnerships and nearly 4.5 million corporations active in the United States. (See Table 1.2.) If each has a buy/sell agreement in place, as they should, and likely do, the number of underlying valuations conducted on an annual basis is exceedingly large.

Table 1.2
Partnerships and Corporations in the United States

	1990	1995
Number of partnerships	1,554,000	1,581,000
Number of corporations	3,717,000	4,474,000

Source: U.S. Department of Commerce, *Statistical Abstract of the United States, 1998*, pp. 543-544.

ACQUISITION OF CAPITAL

From time to time all businesses will be in a position to require additional operating capital. While banks typically do not undertake formal business valuation engagements as part of the loan process, they do perform rather extensive research into the nature of the operations of the business, the internal and external risks facing the company, and the financial strengths and weaknesses of the company. All of these are integral components of any business valuation.

The in-need-of-capital business can acquire capital in one of two ways. The business can issue debt by borrowing money from investors for a specified period of time with the promise to repay the investment at a stated rate of interest and on a stated date. Or, the business can issue equity by borrowing money from investors and in return giving them stock ownership in the business. In either case, a valuation is needed by the business so that investors can study relevant financial data and thereby have a systematic means through which to evaluate the investment opportunity.

In 1996, the latest year for which data are available, corporations acquired operating capital by issuing nearly $550 billion in bonds and more than $100 billion in stocks. (See Table 1.3.) It is intuitive to us that with this volume of capital acquisition need, businesses have a financial incentive to provide accurate valuation information to potential investors, and investors likewise have a financial incentive to require the same.

ESTATE PLANNING

All business owners have at least one partner—Uncle Sam. While he does not attend stockholders' or directors' meetings, while he never participates in company picnics, and while he never assists with the ongoing operations, he is nevertheless entitled to a portion of the annual profits. Not only that, but if the "real" owner of the business sells any of his or her interest in the business, Uncle Sam is entitled to some of those proceeds as well. The real kicker is if the owner gives some of his or her company to another person or if the owner dies while being the owner, Uncle Sam again has the right to be present.

Table 1.3
Capital Acquisitions by U.S. Corporations

	1990	1996
Value of bond offerings	$298.9 billion	$548.9 billion
Value of equity offerings	$40.2 billion	$116.6 billion

Source: U.S. Department of Commerce, *Statistical Abstract of the United States, 1998*, p. 530.

Through estate planning, business owners are able to transfer predetermined amounts of their ownership to their children, or to others, during their lifetime. Because there may be federal and state tax consequences associated with such transfers, it is imperative that the person making the gift have an accurate valuation of the ownership shares being transferred.

Table 1.4 shows the total amount of federal estate and gift taxes collected in both 1990 and 1996, the latest year for which data are available. If the 1996 figure of $18 billion in estate and gift taxes is based on an average estate and gift tax rate of, say 40 percent, the value of such assets is about $45 billion.

Table 1.4
Federal Estate and Gift Taxes

1990	1996
$12 billion	$18 billion

Source: U.S. Department of Commerce, *Statistical Abstract of the United States, 1998*, p. 347.

LITIGATION SUPPORT

The data presented in Table 1.1 through Table 1.4 are, in our opinion, overwhelming in their indirect representation of breadth and scope of business valuation activity throughout the United States. Were similar data also available on the use of business valuations in support of litigation, they would in all likelihood create the same impression. For example, business valuations are at the heart of many equitable distribution disputes, especially if one of the marriage partners holds ownership in a closely held business. In such cases, the ownership share of the closely held business must be valued to determine how to distribute the marital estate. Similarly, business valuations are at the heart of litigation that is related to business interruptions or to unfair business practices. In the former, the economic harm due to a business interruption caused by an outside party is the difference in the value of the business before the interruption and the value of the business after activities resume. In the latter, the economic harm due to unfair business practices is the difference in the value of the business absent the unfair business practice and the current value of the harmed business. Finally, in wrongful death cases or in personal injury cases, the wronged party may suffer a business loss and the valuation of that loss requires that a valuation be done.

THE SCIENCE OF BUSINESS VALUATION

The theme of this book is that business valuation is part art and part science. Those truly experienced in business valuations are not likely to disagree with such a characterization, although they may prefer alternative descriptive terms. The term "judgment" may be preferable by some to the term "art"; the term "systematic" may also be preferred by some to the term "science." Semantics aside, our point is that there are certain elements of business valuation that are readily agreed upon and on which most if not all valuators would not dispute, just as in the appraisal of a home there are certain facts such as square footage that the parties would not dispute. Likewise, there are certain elements about which even the most objective of parties will disagree.

There are many dimensions of the science of business valuation. Listed below are only a few, while many more will be elaborated upon throughout this book. The science of business valuation deals with, among other things, the following:

- adherence of general accounting principles for the organization and presentation of the financial data of the business,
- chronicalization of the facts associated with the historical growth of the business,
- extrapolation of financial data into future time periods, and
- calculation of various valuation ratios and statistical formulae.

These are, without question, critical dimensions to a business valuation, but they are not the only dimensions of a business valuation that are important. All too often, for a variety of reasons, individuals may fall into the trap of believing that business valuation is little more than a formulistic exercise. Nothing, in our opinion, could be further from the truth. In our comparison of the valuation of a business to the appraisal of a home, the more intangible factors that add to the value of the home, such as its architectural style, quality of the school district, and interior floor plan, are part of the art of appraisal and, by analogy, the art of business valuation. Disagreements regarding a final valuation estimate of a business, or the appraisal of a home, are in most cases based on differences in opinion about elements of what we call art.

THE ART OF BUSINESS VALUATION

Just as there are many dimensions of the science of business valuation, there are also many dimensions of the art of business valuation. Listed below are only a few, and, as with the scientific dimensions, many more of these will be elaborated upon throughout this book. The art of business valuation deals with, among other things, the following concepts:

- understanding the economically efficient life of productive assets, compared to the general accounting practice defined depreciable life of productive assets,
- understanding the economically relevant industry in which the business being valued operates,
- understanding the appropriateness of one valuation method or one statistical method over another,
- understanding the limitations of financial information from comparable businesses, and
- understanding the economic environment into which financial data are being extrapolated, and the appropriateness of such an extrapolation.

The reader should not infer from the abbreviated dimensions that we have just listed under the headings of science and art that the practice of accounting as related to business valuation is science and the practice of economics as related to business valuation is art. That is not the case at all. However, a business valuation is often dependent on the ability of the valuator to be knowledgeable of both accounting concepts as well as economic concepts.

Accounting is a systematic way of documenting the business's financial activities, while economics is a systematic way of understanding the market environment in which the business's financial activities take place (and rarely is there a business valuator who is equally versed in both disciplines). Accounting methods are relatively more static in nature than are the economic conditions that surround the business; there are more systematic practices and principles that guide the application of accounting methods than there are that guide economic forecasts. Rarely is there a situation where all aspects of a valuation are accounting related or all aspects are economics related.

OVERVIEW OF THE BOOK

Business valuation is, in our opinion, rapidly becoming a vocation unto itself. Accountants are acquiring education in the field of valuation to serve the needs of their clients better; attorneys are obtaining continuing professional education credits in business valuation issues to represent their clients better; and individuals from various other backgrounds are entering into the profession in response to the growing demand for valuation services. If the reader is contemplating entering the field of business valuation, then this book will provide valuable exposure at the elementary level.

In response to both the growing demand in the field of business valuation, as well as to the associated influx of professionals from myriad backgrounds, we set forth in this book a readable introductory account of various methodologies for valuing a closely held business. We do not, through example or description, universally advocate one valuation method over another. Rather, we describe and critique the appropriateness of several valuation methods. It is not the case that one valuation method is always preferred over another. The selection of appropriate valuation methods requires thought and judgment—the art of business valuation. Our description and critique accounts for both the art and the science that needs to be applied to each of the methods we discuss.

We have yet to see a business valuation that is either total art or total science. We do not believe that any comprehensive valuation can exclude either. We have often been asked when discussing our views on the need for valuation to include both art and science, "Well, how much of a valuation should be art and how much should be science?" The answer to this question is not unexpected, "It depends!" No two valuations—meaning the situations and the attendant methodological considerations about the valuation—are alike. One valuation may have more of a scientific appearance than another, but both will contain aspects of art. Experience will serve a valuator well in balancing the two.

In Chapter 2, we describe basic concepts about a business such as its purpose and the economic environment in which it operates. We describe the accounting methods appropriate for quantifying the extent to which the business fulfills its purpose given the economic environment in which it operates. Finally, we discuss why the business has value.

In Chapter 3, we summarize the basic tools used in a business valuation. These are important elements of the science of business valuation, but we present these tools from a conceptual perspective, to emphasize aspects of art, as well as from a formulistic perspective. We are of the opinion that it is equally important, or perhaps in some circumstances more important, to understand why a formula works as to understand how it works.

Three hypothetical businesses are described in Chapter 4. Certainly, these businesses do not cover the spectrum of all businesses in the U.S. economy, or the spectrum of businesses that the reader will likely valuate over his or her career. Rather, these are three businesses that we constructed in order to facilitate our discussion of the art and science of business valuation. Hence, we emphasize that no generalizations or comparisons should be made between the financial specifics of these hypothetical businesses and particular valuations that a reader may undertake or study.

Chapter 5 discusses, based on the three business examples presented in Chapter 4, several business valuation tools for forecasting financial data. Chapter 6 emphasizes the importance of a thorough understanding of the nature of risk as related to discount rates and capitalization rates. Chapter 7 describes selected approaches to compare the financial performance of one business to other businesses in that industry, and illustrates these approaches in terms of the three business examples in Chapter 4. Chapter 8 overviews alternative valuation methods from a conceptual perspective. Each method is discussed in terms of its underlying assumptions, its relevance to particular valuation exercises, and finally in terms of scientific implementation. Chapters 9 through 11 apply the appropriate valuation methods from Chapter 8 to each of the three business examples in Chapter 4. Chapter 12 concludes the book with summary points about the art and science of business valuation.

2

BASIC CONCEPTS ABOUT A BUSINESS

Money alone sets all the world in motion.
—Syrus

THE PURPOSE OF A BUSINESS

The primary purpose of a business is to make money. This is not an indictment against businesses, and it does not imply that business owners lack altruism or charitableness. It is a fact that the purpose of a business is to make money. Individuals invest resources in a business because they expect a monetary return on their investment.

What about not-for-profit organizations? Of course, by their very nature, not-for-profit organizations are not in business to make money, and by that fact they are definitionally outside the scope of this book. Not-for-profit organizations do not have a need to be valued from the same perspective as do closely held businesses, but certainly such organizations add value to the community in which they operate and to society in general.

If a business does not make a profit, it will eventually cease to exist. How much money must a business make to continue to operate? The answer to this, of course, depends on the return that the owner of the business requires to continue to operate the business. For limited periods of time a business may lose money, but if it has the expectation that it will make enough money in the future to overcome this short-term loss it will continue to operate. Such a situation describes the early-on financial situation of many start-up companies.

Once a business is established, it is reasonable to expect that the owner will continue to operate the business only as long as the business generates a return greater than the return the owner could earn from a comparable alternative investment. Using economic terminology, the owner will continue to operate the business as long as he or she earns an amount that is greater than the opportunity cost of the resources (meaning highest valued alternative use of resources) invested in the business.

An owner may attempt to sell a business because the business is losing or is expected to lose money, or the owner may think that a higher return on investment can be earned elsewhere. To balance this view, one reason that individuals will desire to buy a business is because they believe that they can make more money by operating the business than they can in a comparable alternative investment.

This chapter describes basic concepts that characterize a business. While these basic concepts may appear on the surface to be unrelated, they are very definitely related. The first concept is what we refer to as the economic environment of the business. When we introduce the three businesses that will serve as our illustrative examples for the application of various valuation methods in Chapter 4, the first aspect of each business that we discuss is its economic environment. When we illustrate how to value each of these businesses in Chapters 9, 10, and 11, we again will relate the economic environment of the business to our implementation of a valuation method.

The second concept discussed in this chapter relates to the financial accounting of the business as represented by its income statement and balance sheet. When we characterize, in Chapters 4 and 5, the three businesses that will serve as our examples, we discuss the financial health of each business as reflected on its income statement and balance sheet. Information from the income statement and balance sheet of each business will again be used in Chapter 7 to compare the financial performance of each to its industry and again in the actual valuations in Chapters 9, 10, and 11.

The third concept discussed in this chapter relates to value. A conceptual understanding of value is critical when selecting the appropriate valuation method to apply, as we illustrate in Chapter 9 through 11.

ECONOMIC ENVIRONMENT OF A BUSINESS

Businesses do not operate in isolation from other businesses that produce and sell related goods or services. One key to understanding the economic environment of a business is to understand the meaning of a related product. The word "related" implies that other businesses produce and sell substitutable goods or services. While Company A may believe that its product is unique or markedly better than that produced by any other company, there is still a Company B that makes a product for which, at some price, the consumer will prefer Company B's product over that of Company A's. Two companies do not have to make identical products for the companies to compete with each other, and thus for their products to be substitutable. If there is competition, then the goods or services are substitutable and therefore comparable.

Consider three bakeries in a given geographical area. Bakery A sells only gourmet desserts, made with the finest chocolates and exquisitely decorated. Bakery B sells a quality dessert, although a discriminating palate will quickly discern that its ingredients are somewhat inferior to those used by Bakery A, and its decorations are visibly less elaborate. Bakery C mass produces plebeian-like desserts and sells them far below the prices at either Bakery A or Bakery B. Each bakery probably views its product as distinct and unique, and not a substitute for the products of the other two bakeries.

The economic environment of each bakery is defined, in part, by the presence and actions of the other two bakeries. If Bakery A's prices increase too much, then its customers, while appreciating the quality of its products, will begin to purchase desserts from Bakery B. And so it would be with Bakery B and Bakery C if Bakery B's prices increase too much. Alternatively, if Bakery B introduces a new type of pie in an effort to capture customers from Bakery A and Bakery C, the latter could quickly imitate Bakery B's new product and recapture any temporarily lost customers.

A second key to understanding the economic environment of a business is to understand how outside factors affect either the current or future costs that the business must incur to operate, or the current or future demand that individuals have for the business's product. For example, one factor that is outside the control of a business is a change in the regulatory environment in which the business operates. Consider a case where the government mandates additional environmental and safety regulations. The government could mandate that all bakeries install new ventilation equipment for the safety of workers who are around flour dust for prolonged periods of time. The cost to the business to meet this requirement may raise the operating costs of the bakery to the point that the owner of the business no longer finds it profitable to remain in business. A potential buyer of this business would need to know about this government mandate and must have some insights into the possibility that a similar safety requirement may be mandated in the future. Absent such information this buyer is unable to make a fully informed decision.

On the demand side, unexpected events can have dramatic effects on customers' demand for products. As demand changes, so does the profitability of a business. Recall what happened to the profitability of meat packing plants during the "mad cow disease" scare in 1996. Buyers and sellers alike are subject to unexpected economic events, and the valuation of a business is dependent on whether such events have occurred and the likelihood of such events occurring in the future.

Economic events are not always unexpected. Economic trends are equally important for understanding and forecasting valuation-related activities. For example, there has been a nationwide decrease in the number of individuals who smoke. If this trend continues, and if the government is successful in its efforts to increase the tax on a package of cigarettes, will the value of businesses related to the tobacco industry decrease? Not necessarily so. These trends are domestic, but the U.S. tobacco industry also has a presence in international markets. It may be the case that the international demand for tobacco products would increase faster than the domestic demand would decrease.

Figure 2.1 illustrates the effect of changes in the economic environment of a business on its revenue, and hence on its profitability. Consider a business that produces widgets. The price of widgets is measured in dollars ($) on the vertical axis and the quantity of widgets is measured in units on the horizontal axis. The demand for widgets is shown as a downward sloping line reflecting the fact that at lower prices the quantity that consumers demanded is higher. This demand curve is labeled with the letter D. The supply of widgets is shown as an upward sloping line reflecting the fact that at higher prices the business has an incentive to produce more widgets. This supply curve is labeled with the letter S. (The demand curve, D, and the supply curve, S, are illustrated as straight lines only for graphical simplicity.)

Figure 2.1
Changes in the Economic Environment of Producers of Widgets

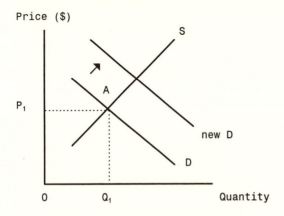

At existing price P_1 this business sells Q_1 amount of widgets and earns revenue equal to Q_1 widgets each being sold at price P_1, or the area defined by $Q_1 \times P_1$. In terms of Figure 2.1, the business earns revenue equal to the area of the rectangle defined by the four points 0, P_1, A, Q_1. If the economic environment related to the demand or the supply of widgets changes, say consumers' demand for widgets increases as shown by the rightward shift in demand curve D to new D, then the price of widgets will increase to a level above P_1 and the quantity produced and sold will increase to a level above Q_1. Revenue, the product of the new price and the new quantity, will increase. A potential seller and a potential buyer both have a need to understand when or if such a phenomenon will occur—and if it does if it will be short-lived or permanent—in order to accurately estimate the value of the business.

INCOME STATEMENTS AND BALANCE SHEETS

An income statement is a conventional format that businesses use to summarize their revenues and costs, the difference between which is net income or profit. It is a scorecard that reflects the financial activity of the business for a period of time, as compared to a balance sheet which is a snapshot reflecting a company's assets and liabilities at a particular point in time. More formally, an income statement presents the financial results of operations for a reporting period—one year in the examples throughout this book. The income statement provides information concerning return on investment, risk, financial flexibility, and operating capabilities. Return on investment is a measure of a business's overall performance in relation to its invested capital. Risk reflects an expectation about the future of the enterprise. Financial flexibility is the business's ability to adapt to problems and opportunities. Operating capability relates to the firm's ability to maintain a given level of operations.

The income statement shows the business's total revenue ($P_1 \times Q_1$ in terms of the diagram in Figure 2.1) and all operating expenses. Table 2.1 is a generic income statement for a professional practice such as a medical practice. Shown in the table are only a few selected items that may be included in operating expenses: physician salaries, the salaries of the other employees such as the nurses and the office staff, the cost of medical supplies, and the depreciated value of the medical equipment. On this income statement, operating expenses are totaled and labeled as Total Operating Expenses. The difference between revenues and operating expenses in this example is net income or profit. The income statement is included in the financial report of a business.

Table 2.1
Generic Income Statement

	Fiscal Year
Revenue	xxx
Operating Expenses	xxx
Physician Salaries	xxx
Other Salaries	xxx
Medical Supplies	xxx
Depreciation	xxx
↓	
Total Operating Expenses	xxx
Net Income	xxx

A balance sheet summarizes the financial position of a business at a point in time. It lists all of the assets and all of the liabilities of the business as of a certain date. More formally, a balance sheet (or statement of financial position) is a report that shows the financial position of the business at a particular moment of time, including the business's economic resources (assets), economic obligations (liabilities), and the residual claims of owners (owners' or stockholders' equity).

A term frequently used by some valuators in their valuation reports is "net assets." Net assets are a company's assets minus its liabilities. Another term for the same amount that is often used by some valuators is "net worth." We typically discourage the use of this latter term since "worth" could be misinterpreted to mean value. Balance sheets prepared under generally accepted accounting principles do not have value as an objective.

Table 2.2 is a generic balance sheet for the medical practice in Table 2.1. Shown in the table are total assets (current assets and depreciable assets), total liabilities, and total stockholders' (owners') equity. Total assets less total liabilities equals, by definition, total stockholders' equity. The balance sheet is included in the financial report of a business.

Table 2.2
Generic Balance Sheet

	Fiscal Year
Current Assets	xxx
Cash	xxx
Accounts Receivable	xxx
↓	
Total Current Assets	xxx
Property and Equipment	xxx
Medical Equipment	xxx
↓	
Total Property and Equipment	xxx
Total Assets	xxx
Current Liabilities	xxx
Accounts Payable	xxx
↓	
Total Current Liabilities	xxx
Stockholders' Equity	xxx
Common Stock	xxx
Retained Earnings	xxx
Total Stockholders' Equity	xxx
Total Liabilities and Equity	xxx

Income statements and balance sheets describe different aspects of a business's financial activities during or at a particular point in time. While both statements can be and often are prepared in a preliminary form each month, our consideration in this book is, as are the considerations of most business valuators, toward a completed fiscal year. For simplicity of exposition, we will view the fiscal year of these three businesses as calendar years, and all of our calculations herein will be based on year-end values.

Also, income statements and balance sheets can be prepared either on an accrual basis or on a cash basis. In accrual accounting, revenues are recognized in the period when they are earned. Expenses and losses are recognized in the period when they are incurred. Accrual-basis accounting is concerned with the economic consequences of events and transactions rather than only with cash receipts and cash payments. Cash-basis accounting recognizes only transactions involving actual cash receipts and disbursement occurring in a given period. Cash-basis accounting recognizes revenues and gains when cash is received and expenses and losses when cash is paid. In our opinion, accrual accounting generally provides the more accurate measure of earnings, earnings power, and managerial performance. All of the examples in this book are presented on an accrual basis.

Lastly, for valuation purposes, income statements and balance sheets will need to be normalized. This process will be discussed in Chapter 7 and illustrated in Chapter 9. While income statements and balance sheets describe the historical financial behavior of a company, for valuation purposes the financial information within them will have to be recast to reflect how a potential buyer might operate the business.

THE VALUE OF A BUSINESS

Regarding business valuations, the term "value" has a number of distinct meanings. We discuss here two meanings, although there are others (for example, intrinsic value or sentimental value). It should also be noted as a word of warning that there are those who apparently view it as their professional calling to develop and exploit semantic nuances associated with the definition of value. That warning having been given, we proceed with what we believe are the two most general definitions of value: fair market value and liquidation value. These two definitions differ, as noted explicitly below, but more important than an understanding of the differences in their definitions is an understanding of the assumptions that underlie their definitions. The assumptions that underlie the definition of value are the same assumptions that are brought to the overall valuation assignment. It is these valuation-relevant assumptions that, in our opinion, determine which definition is relevant to the valuation being conducted, but, the choice of a valuation method, discussed in Chapter 8, depends on which definition of value is appropriate.

Fair Market Value

It may be the case that the vast majority of business valuations conducted relate to a fair market definition of value, although there are no data to substantiate this presumption. Revenue Rulings are published opinions of the Internal Revenue Service regarding various tax issues. Many valuators refer to Revenue Ruling 59-60 as the authority for the definition of fair market value. Revenue Ruling 59-60 deals with valuations of closely held businesses and outlines the approach, methods, and factors to be considered in valuing shares of the capital stock of a closely held corporation for estate tax and gift tax purposes. The Revenue Ruling makes clear that the methods discussed are applicable to the valuation of corporate stocks on which market quotations are unavailable or do not reflect the fair market value. As stated in IRS Revenue Ruling 59-60:

Fair market value [is] the price at which the property would change hands between a willing buyer and a willing seller when the former is not under any compulsion to buy and the latter is not under any compulsion to sell, both parties having reasonable knowledge of the relevant facts.

Before continuing with further discussion on the definition of fair market value, it is important to emphasize again that Revenue Rulings are nothing more than opinions proclaimed by the Internal Revenue Service. Revenue Rulings carry no weight of law. The Internal Revenue Service is challenged routinely on their opinions, and taxpayers routinely prevail when matters are brought to court for a decision. The point is that just because the Internal Revenue Service has an opinion at a particular time that valuations should be performed in a certain way, that opinion should not necessarily limit one's approach to valuations.

As an aside, the Internal Revenue Service adopted Revenue Ruling 59-60 in 1959 in an effort to make explicit the fact that no single simple formula is applicable to the valuation of capital stock:

A determination of fair market value, being a question of fact, will depend upon the circumstance in each case. No formula can be devised that will be generally applicable to the multitude of different valuation issues arising in estate and gift tax cases. . . . A sound valuation will be based upon all relevant facts, but the elements of common sense, informed judgment and reasonableness must enter into the process of weighing those facts and determining their aggregate significance.

In 1965, the Internal Revenue Service issued Revenue Ruling 65-192. Among other things, this ruling broadened valuation concepts, including the definition of fair market value, in Revenue Ruling 59-60 to include more than estate and gift tax matters. Specifically:

The general approach, methods and factors outlined in Revenue Ruling 59-60 . . . for use in closely-held corporate stocks for estate and gift tax purposes are equally applicable to valuations thereof for income and other tax purposes and also in determinations of the fair market values of business interests of any type and of intangible assets for all tax purposes.

Revenue Ruling 59-60 has been modified and amplified numerous times, not only through Revenue Ruling 65-192 but also through Revenue Rulings 65-193, 68-609, 77-287, 80-213, and 83-120. Through all of these revisions, clarifications, and extensions the definition of fair market value has remained as it was in 1959.

The important point to note in this discussion about fair market value is not so much the definition of value per se but rather the implicit assumption underlying the definition. Namely, when determining the fair market value of a business, one is valuing the business as if it were to be sold to a new owner who will continue to operate the business. In other words, the fair market value definition is applicable to a going concern that expects to remain a going concern.

As another aside, some may articulate that the going concern value of a business is distinct from the fair market value of a business. We accept this point of view, but we prefer to think of going concern not as a concept of value but rather as an assumption about the nature of the business being valued.

Liquidation Value

Liquidation is one relief procedure available to an insolvent debtor. Liquidation has as its basic purpose the realization (that is, sale) of assets and the satisfaction of liabilities rather than the continuation of the business. As such, the implicit assumption underlying value defined in terms of liquidation value is that the business's operations will cease and that the assets of the business will be sold, either as an entirety or individually.

It is important to emphasize that the implicit assumption underlying the value of a business defined in terms of fair market value is distinct from the value of a business defined in terms of liquidation value. The two definitions follow from assumptions that are diametrically opposed. Fair market value assumes the business will continue to operate, whereas liquidation value assumes that the business will no longer continue to operate. We emphasize this difference because it has been our experience that some business valuators will assume both of these two alternative definitional possibilities, implement the corresponding two alternative approaches to value the going concern business, and then average the results obtained from each. While such an averaging approach to valuation may provide the valuator with the appearance of being thorough, we believe that such an averaging of approaches is in error because the two approaches are based on mutually exclusive assumptions. Figure 2.2 summarizes these two definitions of value.

Figure 2.2 emphasizes the importance of the relationship between the appropriate definition of value and the implicit assumptions about the life of the business. Particular valuation methods are thus appropriate when it is assumed that a business will continue to operate as opposed to it will cease all operations. This point will be noted in subsequent chapters.

Figure 2.2
Alternative Definitions of Value and Their Underlying Assumptions

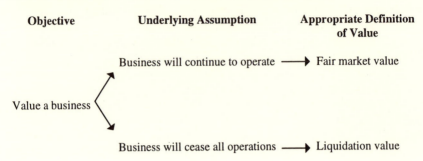

Objective	Underlying Assumption	Appropriate Definition of Value
Value a business	Business will continue to operate ⟶	Fair market value
	Business will cease all operations ⟶	Liquidation value

3

BASIC TOOLS FOR VALUATION

My divine sign indicates the future to me.
—Socrates

INTRODUCTION

The numerical analysis that underlies a business valuation involves a number of quantitative concepts. These concepts are implemented through several mathematical tools. Four of these tools are described in this chapter: forecasting, weighted averages, present value, and capitalization.

There are two important points to note about these four tools. First, they are conceptually related, as will be pointed out in the respective sections of this chapter. Second, the mathematics associated with each tool may appear complicated to some readers, but the looks of mathematics are often deceiving. The concepts underlying each tool are relatively simple, and it is our belief that these underlying concepts must be fully understood so as to implement correctly the tool as well as to understand the interpretative limitations of the tool. Thus, we present the mathematics not to obscure the concept but rather to illustrate the critical assumptions embedded in each concept.

We are of the opinion that one should understand tools before using them. As with the definitions of value in Chapter 2, it is the case that the assumptions brought to a business valuation often dictate the appropriateness of one tool over another.

FORECASTING

Forecasting is a statistical technique that has wide applicability in both business activities and in business valuations. Forecasting involves making judgments about future events based on a systematic analysis of past events and factors that might influence those events in the future. These events and factors generate assumptions that underlie the forecast.

The importance of forecasting to business activities is intuitive. Accurate forecasts of future events can assist owners to make better business decisions in the present. This same idea translates directly to business valuations. A potential buyer will want to know what the business's sales and profits will likely be in the future. A potential seller will want to know similar information before finalizing the decision to sell, much less before setting the sales price.

The most simple forecasting method will extrapolate into the future based on information from the past. One method for extrapolation is to fit a linear trend line to existing information and forecast from that trend line. Fitting a trend line to historical data is part of the science of business valuation; understanding the economic appropriateness and limitations—mathematical limitations and interpretive limitations—of fitting a trend line to historical data and forecasting from it is part of the art of business valuation.

Consider Gate City Widget Company's sales for 1993 through 1997 as reported in Table 3.1. This hypothetical company will be discussed in greater detail later in this book. By inspection of the data in the table, sales have clearly increased each year from 1993 through 1997. Will sales continue to increase in the future? No one knows the answer to this question with 100 percent certainty, but if the past is an indication of the future then the answer is probably yes.

Table 3.1
Gate City Widget Company

Year	Sales
1993	$2,250,000
1994	$2,520,000
1995	$2,822,000
1996	$3,217,000
1997	$3,667,000

Is the past a good predictor for the future? That is the critical question when forecasting future events on the basis of past events. An understanding of the economic environment of the business is fundamental to deciding the appropriateness of such an assumption. If, for example, previous years' sales resulted from unusual and extremely favorable economic conditions, and if the general economic environment has changed since that time, then the past may not be a good predictor of future sales activity. Having emphasized that possibility, we will proceed in this section of this chapter, for simplicity of our introduction of this concept, under the assumption that sales during the 1993 through 1997 period are appropriate elements of information for forecasting future sales. We must reemphasize that this is an assumption for our ease of presentation of forecasting tools. We will question the appropriateness of this assumption in later chapters when we consider in greater detail the valuation of Gate City Widget Company and other businesses.

Fitting a trend line to the sales data in Table 3.1 is based on a statistical technique known as least-squares estimation or least-squares regression analysis. Least squares is the criterion used in regression analysis to define the best straight line to fit a set of data. Certainly, there are a number of straight lines that can approximate a given set of data. The line for which the sum of squared deviations of actual data from fitted data is a minimum (that is, the "least") defines the least-squares line, and it is conventionally accepted that the least-squares line is the "best" line of all possible straight lines to represent a set of data.

While the mathematics associated with fitting a least-squares line is straightforward, it is cumbersome and very unlikely to be calculated by hand. Most computer spreadsheet programs and statistical packages include a regression analysis routine. We will only report regression results herein rather than their derivation.

The results from the least-squares estimation give the equation of the straight line that best fits the data being examined. From this equation, one can determine the average amount by which sales increased each year over the observed time period, and one can use that information to predict sales in the future.

In the case of the sales data in Table 3.1, the estimated least-squares regression equation, as determined from a statistical package, is:

$$\text{Sales} = -701{,}539{,}300 + 353{,}100 \times \text{Year} \tag{3.1}$$

Regardless of the statistical package that is used, equation (3.1) will be the result that is produced by the computer.

The numbers in equation (3.1) result from estimating the regression line that best fits the sales data in Table 3.1. As previously stated, this result can easily be replicated using a computer spreadsheet or a statistical package. What is more important for our purposes is the interpretation of equation (3.1) rather than its derivation. The intercept term is -701,539,300 and the slope term is 353,100. The intercept term is a mathematical construct for the value of sales in unobserved year 0. There is no year 0 in Table 3.1, but since any straight line obviously continues in both directions, there will be a point where the line crosses the vertical axis. More important for our purposes is the numerical value of the slope term, as discussed below. For now, the slope term of 353,100 is interpreted to mean that on average sales increased over the 1993 through 1997 period by $353,100 per year.

More specifically, the estimated regression line in equation (3.1) is interpreted to mean, based on the assumption that sales growth over the past five years was linear, that sales in any future year can be forecast by multiplying the number 353,100 by the numerical representation of the year in question, and then subtracting from that product the number 701,539,300.

Note that these are large numbers. The size of these numbers is directly related to the units of measure of the sales data and of years. Sales data in this case are measured in dollars. Were they measured in thousands of dollars, the magnitude of the regression results—intercept and slope term—would be proportionally smaller. Thus, forecasted sales for 1998, assuming that the previous years' sales are a reasonable predictor of future years' sales, are:

$$\text{Sales}_{1998} = -701,539,300 + (353,100 \times 1998)$$
$$= \$3,954,500 \tag{3.2}$$

Table 3.2 shows the actual values for sales from 1993 through 1997 and the forecast of sales over the years 1998 through 2002. Note in the table that sales increase by \$353,100 each year from 1998 through 2002. Of course, sales could be forecast to any future year, not just over a five-year interval.

Table 3.2
Actual and Trend Line Forecasts of Gate City Widget Company's Sales

Year	Actual Sales	Trend Line Forecast of Sales
1993	\$2,250,000	
1994	\$2,520,000	
1995	\$2,822,000	
1996	\$3,217,000	
1997	\$3,667,000	
1998		\$3,954,500
1999		\$4,307,600
2000		\$4,660,700
2001		\$5,013,800
2002		\$5,366,900

Figure 3.1 is the graphical representative of the sales data in Table 3.2. Actual sales by year are labeled in the figure by an "+" and forecasted sales are represented by the extension of the least-squares regression line through the labeled data points and then beyond 1997 though year 2002. Imposed on the figure is a vertical dotted line referenced to 1998 to emphasize that pre-1998 observations are actual sales data and 1998 through 2002 observations are sales forecasts. These forecasts are mathematically correct given equation (3.1), but these forecasts are relevant to business valuations only if the following two assumptions are valid:

- Sales during the 1993 through 1997 period are an accurate predictor of sales for the next five-year period, with each historical year being given equal weight in the formulation of the forecast.
- Sales in future years will grow in the same linear fashion as they grew over the 1993 through 1997 period.

To the extent that either assumption is incorrect, or less strongly stated, to the extent that either assumption is questionable, then the validity of regression analysis as the appropriate forecasting technique, and consequently the valuation relevance of the forecast of sales values, is likewise questionable.

Figure 3.1
Gate City Widget Company's Actual Sales and Forecast of Sales

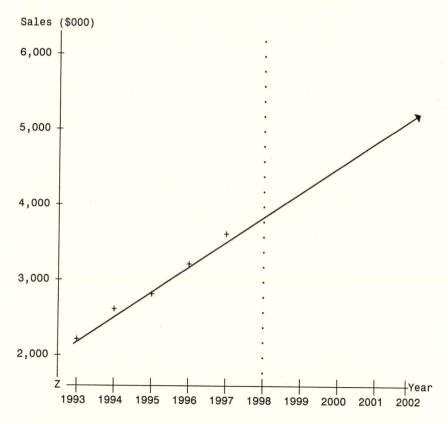

An important, yet subtle point must be explained with regard to equation (3.2) and the associated sales forecasts in Table 3.2 and in Figure 3.1. One may be inclined, based on the least-squares regression results in equation (3.1), to reason in the following way, but one would be in error:

- The slope coefficient in equation (3.1) from the estimated regression line is 353,100.
- The slope coefficient is interpreted to mean that sales increased between 1993 and 1997 at an average of $353,100 per year.
- If sales increased at an average of $353,100 per year over the past five years it is reasonable to expect sales to increase from 1997 to 1998 again by $353,100, assuming that previous years' sales are an accurate predictor of future years' sales.

- Actual sales in 1997 were $3,667,000. If they increase by $353,100 then the forecast of sales for 1998 is $4,020,100 ($3,667,000 + $353,100) as opposed to $3,954,500 as reported in Table 3.2.

The first, second, and the third points are correct. The error occurs with the fourth point. The estimated regression line is the best line that fits all of the historical data based on the least-squares criterion. Thus, it would be the case that the 1997 regression-estimated value of sales, which is on the regression line, should be increased by $353,100 to generate a forecast for 1998. However, the actual 1997 value of sales of $3,667,000 is not on the estimated regression line, and thus it is not the relevant value to use as a base for forecasting in this way. We will revisit this important point in Chapter 5.

An alternative method to fitting a trend line is to extrapolate from previous percentage rates of change in order to infer future percentage rates of change. For example, referring to the actual sales data in either Table 3.1 or Table 3.2, sales increased 12.0 percent between 1993 and 1994, 11.98 percent between 1994 and 1995, 14.0 percent between 1995 and 1996, and 13.99 percent between 1996 and 1997. The average of these four annual percentage rates of increase is 12.99. Thus, one could forecast future sales based on the assumption that future sales will increase at 12.99 per year. (See Table 3.3.) Based on 1997 sales of $3,667,000, 1998 sales are forecast to be 12.99 percent greater, or $4,143,343. This predicted value is slightly higher than the value forecast from the fitted trend line in equation (3.1) and equation (3.2) of $3,954,500.

Table 3.3
Actual and Percentage Growth Forecasts of Gate City Widget Company's Sales

Year	Actual Sales	Percentage Growth Forecast of Sales
1993	$2,250,000	
1994	$2,520,000	
1995	$2,822,000	
1996	$3,217,000	
1997	$3,667,000	
1998		$4,143,343
1999		$4,681,564
2000		$5,289,699
2001		$5,976,831
2002		$6,753,221

There is no a priori way to determine if trend line forecasting will produce a higher or a lower value than average percentage growth forecasting. That, as should be expected, depends on the pattern of the historical data being analyzed. However, obtaining a higher or a lower value certainly is not the relevant issue. What is fundamental to either of these forecasting techniques is the assumption that the pattern of previous years' sales is an accurate predictor of the pattern of future years' sales. To the extent that this assumption is inaccurate, any forecast value will likewise be inaccurate.

Which forecasting technique is better, the trend line forecast or the average annual percentage growth forecast? Both forecasts are based on the assumption that the past mirrors the future. Trend line analysis follows from the additional assumption that the future is a linear projection of the past. Also, the average annual percentage growth forecast mathematically ensures that the annual percentage growth in future years will not be greater than the largest annual percentage growth in previous years. Thus, the answer to this question centers on the appropriateness of the assumptions.

We will revisit each technique in Chapter 5, but here we emphasize again that forecasting techniques, like all business valuation techniques, are based on implicit assumptions, and it is the assumptions that must mirror reality for the technique to be used meaningfully.

WEIGHTED AVERAGES

An average is a measure of central tendency. Three common measures of central tendency are the mean, median (the value in the middle), and mode (the most frequently observed value). Most people think of an average and a mean as being synonymous, the mean is an average but not the only average that can be calculated from a given set of data. The calculation of a mean value is simple; add up the values and divide by the number of values.

For example, the mean of the five sales values in Table 3.1 is $2,895,200. This mean value was calculated by adding together the five values (sum = $14,476,000) and then dividing that sum by 5. Underlying this mean value calculation is an explicit weight of 1 for each of the five values. In other words, sales in 1993 are weighted or treated in the calculation the same as sales in 1994, and so on. This constant unit weighting occurs for each value of sales over the five-year period. See Table 3.4 for the mathematical specifics of this calculation.

If one can substantiate the assumption that all five years of sales data are equally important for characterizing the expected future sales of Gate City Widget Company, then the analysis in Table 3.4 is valid to use for forecasting future sales. However, if one has additional information that, say, would lead to the conclusion that sales activity in 1997 is the most representative year of the five and 1993 is the least representative year, then weighting each year equally, as in the calculation of a mean on the basis of Table 3.4, does not reflect that reality. One of several alternative weighting approaches could alternatively be used. For example, one could weight 1994 sales twice as much as 1993 sales, weight 1995 sales three times as much as 1993 sales, weight 1996 sales four times as much as 1993 sales, and weight 1997 sales five times as much as 1993 sales. Thus, as shown in Table 3.5, the weighted average of sales under this particular, and frequently used, weighting scheme is the sum of the weighted sales figures divided by the sum of the weights.

Table 3.4
Average of Gate City Widget Company's Sales

Year	Actual Sales	Weight	Weighted Sales
1993	$2,250,000	1	$ 2,250,000
1994	$2,520,000	1	$ 2,520,000
1995	$2,822,000	1	$ 2,822,000
1996	$3,217,000	1	$ 3,217,000
1997	$3,667,000	1	$ 3,667,000
Total		5	$14,476,000

Weighted Average = $14,476,000/5 = $2,895,200

Table 3.5
Weighted Average of Gate City Widget Company's Sales

Year	Actual Sales	Weight	Weighted Sales
1993	$2,250,000	1	$ 2,250,000
1994	$2,520,000	2	$ 5,040,000
1995	$2,822,000	3	$ 8,466,000
1996	$3,217,000	4	$12,868,000
1997	$3,667,000	5	$18,335,000
Total		15	$46,959,000

Weighted Average = $46,959,000/15 = $3,130,600

The calculation of the weighted average of sales in Table 3.5 is straightforward, as shown in equation 3.3:

$$\text{Weighted Average} = [(\$2,250,000 \times 1) + (\$2,520,000 \times 2) + (\$2,822,000 \times 3)$$
$$+ (\$3,217,000 \times 4) + (\$3,667,000 \times 5)]/15$$
$$= \$46,959,000/15$$
$$= \$3,130,600 \tag{3.3}$$

Thus, the weighted average of Gate City Widget Company's sales based on the 5-4-3-2-1 weighing scheme is $3,130,600, compared to the mean value based on the 1-1-1-1-1 weighting scheme of $2,895,200.

As we will discuss in later chapters, weighted averages are often used as base values for forecasting future financial events. The 5-4-3-2-1 weighting scheme is conventional, but this fact does not imply that such a weighting scheme is appropriate for every valuation. The particular economic environment of the business should determine if a weighted average calculation is relevant, and then if so the environment should influence the weights to apply to the values being averaged as well as the number of years to include in the averaging procedure. Determining the weights to use in the calculation of a weighted average is art; doing the associated calculations is science.

While weighted averages are in themselves not a forecasting technique, certain valuation approaches, as discussed throughout the book, are based on weighted average values. Mathematically, a weighted average of a set of data can never be greater than the largest datum. In other words, the weighted average of the actual sales in Table 3.5 is $3,130,600. This value is less than the actual sales in either 1996 or 1997. Our point is that if one has prior information from which to conclude that sales are expected to increase in the future, then the use of weighted averages may be inappropriate.

PRESENT VALUE

What is the value today of $1 that a person has today? Obviously, the present value of the $1 that the person has today is $1. What is the value today of $1 that a person is expected to have one year from now? Or, to rephrase the question, how much would a person pay today for the right to have $1 one year from now?

Jumping ahead, how much would one pay today for Gate City Widget Company if, hypothetically, it is expected to be worth $1,000,000 one year from now? Obviously, the answer is less than $1,000,000 but the amount less depends on the rate of return that can be earned if the purchase price is invested in comparable alternative investments. For example, if one could earn 10 percent from a comparable alternative investment, one would not pay $995,000 today for a business that will be worth $1,000,000 one year from now because one could invest the $995,000 and earn a 10 percent rate of return. At the end of one year, one would have from this alternative investment $1,094,500 ($995,000 + 10%), which is more than the $1,000,000 value of the business. (Please note our use of the word "comparable" to characterize the alternative investment in this scenario. We will discuss why the alternative investment must be comparable in Chapter 6.)

Based on this hypothetical example, a key element in the determination of the value of a future asset is the availability of comparable alternative investment opportunities. If the alternative investment opportunity is expected to earn an annual rate, r, then r is called in present value analysis the discount rate or rate at which a future value is to be referenced to the present.

The science of present value calculations is simple; the art is not. Approximating the comparable alternative investment opportunities involves art because such opportunities must indeed be comparable, that is, characterized by the same level of risk as the future asset is being valued.

Regarding science, let PV represent present value and let r represent the discount rate, or the alternative annual rate of return that has been determined to be comparable. Let the value of the asset one year in the future be $X. Then, the present value of $X is represented as:

$$PV = \$X/(1 + r)^1 \tag{3.4}$$

The logic of equation (3.4) is that PV amount of money can be invested for one year at rate r to earn $X. At the end of one year this investor will have the amount originally invested, PV, plus the interest earned on that investment. Multiplying both sides of equation (3.4) by $(1 + r)^1$:

$$PV \times (1 + r)^1 = \$X, \text{ or}$$
$$PV + rPV = \$X \tag{3.5}$$

At the end of one year this investor will have the amount originally invested, PV, and the interest earned on that investment, rPV. So, at the end of one year the investor will have $X. $X is the one-year future value of an investment of PV dollars now to earn interest at the rate, r. Or, PV is the present value of $X one year in the future discounted at the rate, r.

The superscript notation of 1 in equation (3.4) or equation (3.5) refers to the fact that the time horizon is one year into the future. If the time horizon were two years into the future, then the superscript would be 2, and so on; and, $(1 + r)^2$ equals $(1 + r) \times (1 + r)$.

Table 3.6 illustrates several hypothetical present value calculations. Several patterns are noteworthy from the table. One pattern observed in the upper portion of the table is that for a given discount rate, there is an inverse relationship between present value and the time horizon. As shown in the upper portion of the table, for a discount rate of 10 percent, the present value of $100 one year from now is $90.91; the present value of $100 two years from now is $82.64; and the present value of $100 three years from now is $75.13. One may generalize that the longer the period a future asset is being discounted, the smaller the present value of that future asset. The logic of this generalized relationship is that a smaller present value is needed today because it has a longer period to increase in value by earning at the rate, r.

Table 3.6
Present Value of $100 Discounted for n Years at Discount Rate r

Year, n	Discount Rate, r	Present Value, PV
1	.10	$90.91
2	.10	$82.64
3	.10	$75.13
2	.10	$82.64
2	.20	$69.44
2	.30	$59.17

The second pattern observed from the lower portion of the table is that for a given time horizon, there is an inverse relationship between present value and the value of the discount rate. As shown, for a time horizon of two years, the present value of $100 discounted at 10 percent per year is $82.64; the present value when discounted at 20 percent per year for two years is $69.44; and when the discount rate is 30 percent the present value is $59.17. One may thus generalize that, for a given time horizon, the larger the discount rate the smaller the present value of the future asset. The logic of this relationship is that a significant discount rate implies a large alternative investment opportunity, and a smaller present value is needed because it will increase at a larger rate each year.

The concept of present value not only applies to a single asset n years in the future, but it also applies to a continuous stream of assets. For example, the present value of a stream of $100,000 in each of the next ten years, discounted at the rate r, is mathematically represented as:

$$PV = [\$100,000/(1 + r)^1] + [\$100,000/(1 + r)^2] + \dots + [\$100,000/(1 + r)^9]$$
$$+ [\$100,000/(1 + r)^{10}] \tag{3.6}$$

This example is useful if one were to value a business in terms of its ability to generate profit in future years. If the investor's planning horizon is ten years, as is explicit in equation (3.6), and if the business is expected to generate $100,000 in profits in each of the next ten years, then a reasonable first approximation to the value of the business is the present value of a ten-year stream of $100,000 amounts, discounted at the rate, r.

A useful mathematical shortcut (presented here without derivation) for calculations like that in equation (3.6), where the horizon is a finite period of n years, is:

$$PV = \$100,000 \{[(1 + r)^n - 1]/[r(1 + r)^n]\} \tag{3.7}$$

CAPITALIZATION

Capitalization refers to the process of calculating the present value of an infinite steam of constant value assets at the discount rate, r. In terms of equation (3.6), assume that the business is expected to last forever rather than for only ten years, and that in each future year the business is expected to earn $100,000. The present value of this infinite (∞) stream of profits is:

$$PV = [\$100,000/(1 + r)^1] + \dots + [\$100,000/(1 + r)^\infty] \tag{3.8}$$

In equation (3.8), the $100,000 is in each of the terms being summed from year 1 through year ∞. Thus, $100,000 can be factored from each term in equation (3.8), and the equation can be rewritten as:

$$PV = \$100,000 \{[1/(1 + r)^1] + \dots + [1/(1 + r)^\infty]\} \tag{3.9}$$

The expression in braces in equation (3.9) is mathematically equivalent to $[1/r]$ (presented here without derivation), which is called the capitalization factor. Thus, given this equivalency, equation (3.9) becomes:

$PV = \$100,000 \,[1/r]$, or
$PV = \$100,000/r$ (3.10)

Equation (3.10) follows logically from equation (3.7). As the time horizon increases, that is, as n approaches ∞, in equation (3.7) the numerator in the first bracketed expression approaches $[(1 + r)^n]$. Thus, the term in braces in equation (3.7) in this limiting situation equals $\{[(1 + r)^n]/r(1 + r)^n]\}$. After canceling like-terms, this expression becomes $[1/r]$.

The discount rate is r in each of the above present value calculations. When the time horizon is infinite, it is common for the discount rate to be referred to as the capitalization rate or informally as simply the "cap" rate. The corresponding capitalization factor is thus the reciprocal of the capitalization rate.

Referring to equation (3.10), if the capitalization rate is 10 percent or .10, then the capitalization factor is $[1/.10]$ or 10; if the capitalization rate is 20 percent, then the capitalization factor is $[1/.20]$ or 5. For the latter, the present value of an infinite \$100,000 stream of annual profits is \$500,000.

It is important to emphasize that the implicit assumption that underlies capitalization is that the asset being present valued has an infinite life. That is, the implicit assumption is that the asset will last forever and always remain at the same value. If the valuator capitalizes financial data for business valuation purposes, then the implicit assumption is interpreted to mean that the business will last forever; it will generate the exact same financial data in each and every year—forever. If such an assumption is unrealistic, then using a capitalization approach to valuation will yield results that may also be unrealistic.

4

THREE BUSINESSES IN NEED OF VALUATION

Example is always more efficacious than precept.
—Samuel Johnson

INTRODUCTION

Every business valuation is unique in some regard. It may be that the business being valued is itself unique. Perhaps the business manufactures a product that is distinctively different from any product being produced by any competitors. Perhaps the business's owners have special management or leadership qualities that are not replicated by any other owner in the industry and cannot be replicated by a potential owner. Perhaps the economic environment surrounding the business is expected to change in a unique way in the near future, and this change will alter the competitive strategy pursued by the owner. This hypothetical list of unique characteristics or unique events could go on and on.

In this chapter we present three distinctively different businesses in terms of the products that they provide. Our goal throughout this book is to emphasize, through example, both the art and the science of business valuation as we illustrate alternative valuation methods, and to discuss the appropriateness of one method over another. The three hypothetical businesses that we consider are Gate City Widget Company, which manufactures widgets; Gate City Video Rental; which generates its revenue from retail video rentals; and Gate City Orthopedic Clinic, which provides orthopedic surgery and extended medical care. Of course, these businesses and their financial statuses have been constructed and should not be interpreted to represent a norm or a benchmark against which readers of this book will compare their own businesses or the businesses that they may be valuing. However, each business does mirror in the most general sense similar businesses that we have valued.

For simplicity purposes, assume that each of the three businesses reports on the accrual basis, and each has a fiscal year running from January 1 through December 31. We also assume that the relevant financial statements are accurate and conform to generally accepted accounting practices.

We summarize in this chapter background information about each company. Our summary begins with an overview of the economic environment of each business. Although the businesses are hypothetical, our description of the economic environment of each is accurate. It draws on information in the annual U.S. Department of Commerce publication entitled *U.S. Industry & Trade Outlook, 1998,* a reference that all business valuators should consider consulting when studying the economic environment of a business. We also discuss selected aspects of the financial condition of each business, although that element of valuation is dealt with in greater detail in Chapter 7 and then again in Chapters 9 through 11 where each business is valued.

GATE CITY WIDGET COMPANY

A widget is an informal term for a gadget. For purposes of this example, this company's widgets are used in making machine tools. Gate City Widget Company was founded in 1951 by William E. Warner. He has been the company's only president and is the only stockholder. The company's income statement covering the last five years is reproduced in Table 4.1 and its balance sheet for this same time period is reproduced in Table 4.2.

As with any valuation, it is critical to inspect the income statement and the balance sheet for patterns of activity, be these patterns regular or irregular. An inspection of the income statement shows that sales have increased in a regular manner over the last five years. In 1993 total sales were $2,250,000 and in 1997 they were $3,667,000, thus sales increased a total of 63 percent over this five-year period. Associated with this growth in sales has been a cumulative rate of growth in net income of 611 percent. A more complete statistical analysis of these growth trends is presented in Chapter 5.

The balance sheets similarly depict a company in steady-state growth over this five-year period. The business is generating a significant amount of cash. Also, it operates with relatively little capital equipment. The book value of the equipment was only $395,000 in 1997. Regarding liabilities, the company has no long-term debt and few other liabilities. This relationship between total assets and total current liabilities has been stable, and retained earnings have grown steadily over this five-year period.

Gate City Widget Company sells its widgets throughout the southeastern United States. While there are numerous other widget companies in this region of the country, Gate City Widget has a loyal customer base and regards few of the other regional companies as viable competitors. However, this favorable geographic competitive position is not the primary reason behind the company's growth in sales or profitability. The more relevant aspects of the economic environment of the company for business valuation purposes are not related to its domestic market but rather to the international market, namely the international demand for widgets by manufacturers of machine tools.

Table 4.1
Gate City Widget Company: Income Statement

	1993	1994	1995	1996	1997
Sales	$2,250,000	$2,520,000	$2,822,000	$3,217,000	$3,667,000
Cost of Goods Sold	1,350,000	1,512,000	1,693,000	1,930,000	2,200,000
Gross Profit	900,000	1,008,000	1,129,000	1,287,000	1,467,000
Operating Expenses:					
Officers' Compensation	175,000	189,000	204,000	220,000	238,000
Other Salaries	300,000	324,000	350,000	378,000	408,000
Payroll Taxes	40,000	44,000	47,000	51,000	55,000
Profit Sharing Plan	45,000	47,000	49,000	51,000	54,000
Office Supplies	30,000	32,000	35,000	38,000	41,000
Depreciation	25,000	30,000	35,000	40,000	45,000
Rent	125,000	125,000	125,000	125,000	125,000
Insurance	38,000	40,000	42,000	44,000	46,000
Office Supplies	25,000	26,000	27,000	28,000	29,000
Other Expenses	50,000	26,000	83,000	83,000	92,000
Total Operating Expenses	853,000	883,000	997,000	1,058,000	1,133,000
Net Income	$ 47,000	$ 125,000	$ 132,000	$ 229,000	$ 334,000

The following trends are relevant. Domestic growth in machine tools between 1993 and 1997 averaged 9 percent per year, although domestic growth
began to slow in 1996 and 1997. The international demand for machine tools, in
contrast, increased nearly 20 percent per year over this 1993 to 1997 time period. Gate City Widget is fortunate to have negotiated in 1990 several secure
long-term contracts with major Asian companies, and these contractual relationships have accounted for the majority of the growth in its sales and the associated growth in its net income. In addition, the company initiated several labor-
saving production techniques that accounted for the more rapid growth in its
profits compared to its sales.

The future looks promising for Gate City Widget Company. While domestic demand for machine tools is forecast to decline over the next few years, this
domestic decline will be more than offset by strong international growth, especially in the Asian markets. Thus, the industry should enjoy a moderate 5 to 6
percent annual rate of growth in sales through the year 2002, and the company
should outperform the industry due to its international ties in the future.

Table 4.2
Gate City Widget Company: Balance Sheet

	1993	1994	1995	1996	1997
Current Assets:					
Cash	$ 55,000	$ 75,000	$ 115,000	$ 205,000	$ 165,000
Accounts Receivable	325,000	373,000	425,000	568,000	753,000
Inventory	445,000	490,000	549,000	571,000	799,000
Prepaid Expenses	2,500	2,500	2,500	2,500	2,500
Total Current Assets	827,500	940,500	1,091,500	1,346,500	1,719,500
Property and Equipment:					
Manufacturing Equipment	425,000	500,000	540,000	565,000	595,000
Office Furniture and Equipment	75,000	80,000	95,000	110,000	125,000
Accumulated Depreciation	(175,000)	(205,000)	(240,000)	(280,000)	(325,000)
Total Property and Equipment	325,000	375,000	395,000	395,000	395,000
Total Assets	$1,152,500	$1,315,500	$1,486,500	$1,741,500	$2,114,500
Current Liabilities:					
Accounts Payable	$ 175,000	$ 193,000	$ 212,000	$ 233,000	$ 256,000
Bank Loan—Line of Credit	155,000	170,000	185,000	185,000	195,000
Accrued Salaries	20,000	21,000	22,000	23,000	24,000
Accrued Profit Sharing Contribution	45,000	47,000	49,000	51,000	54,000
Other Accrued Liabilities	20,000	22,000	24,000	26,000	28,000
Total Current Liabilities	415,000	453,000	492,000	518,000	557,000
Stockholders' Equity:					
Common Stock	10,000	10,000	10,000	10,000	10,000
Retained Earnings	727,500	852,500	984,500	1,213,500	1,547,500
Total Stockholders' Equity	737,500	862,500	994,500	1,223,500	1,557,500
Total Liabilities and Equity	$1,152,500	$1,315,500	$1,486,500	$1,741,500	$2,114,500

Growth in sales is expected to increase in future years for at least three specific reasons. First, the company's widgets are integral to the robots being used in machine tool operations, and the export of machine tools is expected to increase over the next five years at between 15 and 20 percent per year. Second, U.S. machine tool builders are strategically positioned to introduce new generations of machine tools as soon as the year 2000. When this occurs, the domestic demand for widgets will increase, and Gate City Widget's competitive position in the southeastern United States will serve it well. Third, a major concern for the metalworking industry in general and the machine tool industry in particular is environmental standards and regulations. Environmental issues relate to the disposal of hazardous chemicals used in production. Most machine tool manufacturers have adopted new technologies to minimize the use of such fluids, and Gate City Widget's customers are some of the few machine tool companies that are at the forefront of meeting these regulations. As such, these customers are well positioned in the market to respond quickly and efficiently to increases in domestic demand.

Warner desires to have his company valued for estate planning purposes. He would like, over the next several years, to gift shares of the company to each of his three children.

GATE CITY VIDEO RENTAL

Gate City Video Rental opened the first of its six stores in 1990. The business is owned and operated by Stanley Starling and Frederick Frost, who are equal partners.

As the company's income statement in Table 4.3 reveals, revenues from movie rentals have increased slowly but steadily over the past five years; however, total operating expenses have increased more rapidly. The net income of Gate City Video Rental has fallen from $138,000 in 1993 to a loss of $130,000 in 1997, as would be expected when operating expenses grow faster than revenues. Its balance sheet is in Table 4.4.

As calculated from Table 4.3, revenues from rentals increased at an average annual rate of 9 percent. However, in contrast to such revenue growth, profits fell nearly 49 percent per year, becoming negative in 1996. This decline in net income was due to an increase in operating expenses. In particular, the cost of movies increased at an average annual rate of 9 percent, thus offsetting revenue increases, but also owners' salaries (officers' compensation) have increased at an average rate of nearly 12 percent per year.

The economic environment surrounding Gate City Video Rental is characterized by competing technologies more so than by competing video rental stores. Although the company has expanded its number of stand-alone stores, it continues to face competition from other super video rental stores as well as from food stores that have begun to rent videos. More important, especially for valuing the company, the growth in competing technologies causes one to question the economic life of video cassette technology and hence to question the economic life of the video rental industry as a whole.

There are two important competing technologies that will have a forceful competitive impact on the video rental industry over the next five years. The first is cable television and the second is satellite dish reception. As more telephone company cable providers replace their coaxial cable with optical fibers, the quality of cable television will improve and the breadth of available programming will expand. As well, with this expansion in delivery capabilities, pay-per-view programming will rival video rentals because current releases will be available sooner and at a lower price (especially when one considers in the total price of a video rental not only the rental price at the counter but also the time needed to travel to and from the video store).

Table 4.3
Gate City Video Rental: Income Statement

	1993	1994	1995	1996	1997
Movie Rentals	$2,200,000	$2,376,000	$2,566,000	$2,771,000	$2,993,000
Operating Expenses:					
Cost of Movies Rented	770,000	832,000	898,000	970,000	1,048,000
Officers' Compensation	250,000	275,000	303,000	333,000	366,000
Other Salaries	625,000	688,000	757,000	795,000	811,000
Payroll Taxes	74,000	82,000	90,000	96,000	100,000
Profit Sharing Plan	30,000	32,000	34,000	36,000	38,000
Office Supplies	30,000	32,000	35,000	38,000	41,000
Depreciation	25,000	30,000	35,000	40,000	45,000
Rent	145,000	157,000	170,000	184,000	199,000
Insurance	38,000	40,000	42,000	44,000	46,000
Office Supplies	25,000	26,000	27,000	28,000	29,000
Other Expenses	50,000	65,000	119,000	221,000	400,000
Total Operating Expenses	2,062,000	2,259,000	2,510,000	2,785,000	3,123,000
Net Income	$ 138,000	$ 117,000	$ 56,000	($ 14,000)	($130,000)

Since 1995, the price of small 18-inch receiving dishes has fallen, while growth in demand has risen. Through year 2000, the projected growth in subscribers to this media is about 36 percent per year. Direct-to-home satellite broadcasting is a technology that is more infant than beamed satellite technology, but one that is expected to be more affordable within the next five years. As well, satellite technology will offer subscribers a wider range of viewing options than are now available via coaxial cable connections or even via optical fiber connections. Increases in subscribers to both satellite and improved cable capabilities will come at the expense of video rentals.

Starling and Frost desire to have their rental business valued because Starling wants to retire and sell his interest in the business to Frost. Frost plans to sell, or more likely to liquidate, the business shortly thereafter.

Table 4.4
Gate City Video Rental: Balance Sheet

	1993	1994	1995	1996	1997
Current Assets:					
Cash	$ 25,000	$ 65,000	$105,000	$115,000	$ 75,000
Movie Inventory	250,000	300,000	336,000	349,000	314,000
Prepaid Expenses	2,500	2,500	2,500	2,500	2,500
Total Current Assets	277,500	367,500	443,500	466,500	391,500
Property and Equipment:					
Leasehold Improvements	250,000	300,000	340,000	370,000	390,000
Office Furniture and Equipment	95,000	140,000	155,000	170,000	185,000
Accumulated Depreciation	(75,000)	(105,000)	(140,000)	(180,000)	(225,000)
Total Property and Equipment	270,000	335,000	355,000	360,000	350,000
Total Assets	$547,500	$702,500	$798,500	$826,500	$741,500
Current Liabilities:					
Accounts Payable	$200,000	$220,000	$242,000	$266,000	$293,000
Bank Loan—Line of Credit	175,000	190,000	205,000	220,000	235,000
Accrued Salaries	15,000	16,000	17,000	18,000	19,000
Accrued Profit Sharing Contribution	30,000	32,000	34,000	36,000	38,000
Other Accrued Liabilities	15,000	15,000	15,000	15,000	15,000
Total Current Liabilities	435,000	473,000	513,000	555,000	600,000
Stockholders' Equity:					
Common Stock	10,000	10,000	10,000	10,000	10,000
Retained Earnings	102,500	219,500	275,500	261,500	131,500
Total Stockholders' Equity	112,500	229,500	285,500	271,500	141,500
Total Liabilities and Equity	$547,500	$702,500	$798,500	$826,500	$741,500

GATE CITY ORTHOPEDIC CLINIC

Doctor Bruce Breslow opened Gate City Orthopedic in 1977, having previously been on the surgical staff at Gate City Hospital. The clinic has done very well in the past few years. Patient revenues have increased at an average annual rate of 9 percent, while net income has grown at nearly 24 percent per year, as shown in Table 4.5. This increase in patient revenue has come primarily from new patient growth rather than increases in patient charges. In fact, in recent years revenue per patient visit has decreased, as discussed below. The company's balance sheet is in Table 4.6.

Table 4.5
Gate City Orthopedic Clinic: Income Statement

	1993	1994	1995	1996	1997
Patient Revenues	$1,700,000	$1,836,000	$1,983,000	$2,142,000	$2,313,000
Operating Expenses:					
Physicians' Compensation	650,000	715,000	787,000	866,000	953,000
Other Salaries	325,000	358,000	394,000	433,000	476,000
Payroll Taxes	70,000	77,000	85,000	94,000	103,000
Profit Sharing Plan	85,000	89,000	93,000	98,000	103,000
Cafeteria Plan	45,000	49,000	53,000	57,000	62,000
Medical Supplies	60,000	65,000	70,000	76,000	82,000
Office Supplies	30,000	32,000	35,000	38,000	41,000
Depreciation	40,000	40,000	40,000	40,000	40,000
Rent	75,000	75,000	75,000	75,000	75,000
Malpractice Insurance	110,000	116,000	122,000	128,000	134,000
Other Insurance	45,000	47,000	49,000	51,000	54,000
Office Supplies	25,000	26,000	27,000	28,000	29,000
Bad Debts	40,000	40,000	40,000	40,000	40,000
Other Expenses	50,000	32,000	31,000	29,000	24,000
Total Operating Expenses	1,650,000	1,761,000	1,901,000	2,053,000	2,216,000
Net Income	$ 50,000	$ 75,000	$ 82,000	$ 89,000	$ 97,000

The competitive environment that characterizes the health care industry has changed significantly since 1977, and it may change even more during the next decade. It is best described by the phrase "managed care," meaning a system of prepaid plans for providing comprehensive coverage to members. The alleged benefit of a managed health care is that it controls the use of health services by patients in order to provide a most cost-effective delivery of these services. Managed health care plans seek to partner with health care providers that are willing to provide on a contractual basis low-cost care in return for a defined patient base. Currently, over 70 percent of all physicians in the United States operate their practices under managed care, and this percentage is growing.

Table 4.6
Gate City Orthopedic Clinic: Balance Sheet

	1993	1994	1995	1996	1997
Current Assets:					
Cash	$ 25,000	$ 35,000	$ 45,000	$ 55,000	$ 65,000
Accounts Receivable	776,000	854,000	939,000	1,033,000	1,136,000
Prepaid Expenses	2,500	2,500	2,500	2,500	2,500
Total Current Assets	803,500	891,500	986,500	1,090,500	1,203,500
Property and Equipment:					
Medical Equipment	225,000	255,000	285,000	315,000	345,000
Office Furniture and Equipment	95,000	110,000	125,000	140,000	155,000
Accumulated Depreciation	(135,000)	(175,000)	(215,000)	(255,000)	(295,000)
Total Property and Equipment	185,000	190,000	195,000	200,000	205,000
Total Assets	$988,500	$1,081,500	$1,181,500	$1,290,500	$1,408,500
Current Liabilities:					
Accounts Payable	$ 55,000	$ 61,000	$ 67,000	$ 74,000	$ 81,000
Accrued Salaries	150,000	158,000	166,000	174,000	183,000
Accrued Profit Sharing Contribution	85,000	89,000	93,000	98,000	103,000
Other Accrued Liabilities	15,000	15,000	15,000	15,000	15,000
Total Current Liabilities	305,000	323,000	341,000	361,000	382,000
Stockholders' Equity:					
Common Stock	10,000	10,000	10,000	10,000	10,000
Retained Earnings	673,500	748,500	830,500	919,500	1,016,500
Total Stockholders' Equity	683,500	758,500	840,500	929,500	1,026,500
Total Liabilities and Equity	$988,500	$1,081,500	$1,181,500	$1,290,500	$1,408,500

Managed health care limits the revenue potential of a given practice because payments are based on a preestablished fee schedule. As a result, there is a financial incentive for managed health care practices, especially those with one or only a few physicians, to merge or consolidate in order to achieve economies of scale in the provision of their services. In addition, hospitals are increasingly acquiring practices in order to achieve economies of scale and scope in the services that they provide, as well as controlling the referral of patients.

Breslow is the primary physician at the clinic and owns 100 percent of the stock in the corporation. Two other physicians are on staff, each working about thirty hours per week. Breslow desires to have his practice valued in anticipation of the opportunity to sell one-third of his practice to each of the other physicians.

Subsequent chapters will revisit these three companies. In those chapters each of the three companies will be valued, and in the process we will illustrate alternative valuation methods.

5

TRENDS IN FINANCIAL DATA

Annual income twenty pounds, annual expenditure nineteen nineteen
six, result happiness.
Annual income twenty pounds, annual expenditure twenty pounds
ought and six, result misery.
—Charles Dickens

INTRODUCTION

We introduced in Chapter 3 several basic tools used by business valuators when examining financial data—forecasting, weighted averages, present value, and capitalization. We emphasized in Chapter 4 the importance of inspecting the financial data that will be studied at the beginning of the valuation exercise so as to better understand trends in the business's activities and any idiosyncratic activities that may have occurred in recent years vis-à-vis the economic environment of the business. In this chapter we bridge the ideas, and we illustrate the application of two of the basic tools previously discussed—forecasting and weighted averages—as a formal introduction to the statistical aspects of the valuation of Gate City Widget Company, Gate City Video Rental, and Gate City Orthopedic Clinic in Chapters 9, 10, and 11, respectively.

We begin by reproducing selected parts of the income statement and the balance sheet for each of these three businesses. For Gate City Widget Company these portions are in Table 5.1 and Table 5.2, for Gate City Video Rental these are in Table 5.3 and Table 5.4, and for Gate City Orthopedic Clinic these are in Table 5.5 and Table 5.6. The three financial measures that we have selected for analysis in this chapter are sales or revenues, net income, and stockholders' equity. These are only three of the many important financial measures that are scrutinized when conducting a business valuation, but in our opinion they are among those that are most likely to be forecast.

Table 5.1
Gate City Widget Company: Selected Items from the Income Statement

	1993	1994	1995	1996	1997
Sales	$2,250,000	$2,520,000	$2,822,000	$3,217,000	$3,667,000
Net Income	$ 47,000	$ 125,000	$ 132,000	$ 229,000	$ 334,000

Table 5.2
Gate City Widget Company: Selected Items from the Balance Sheet

	1993	1994	1995	1996	1997
Stockholders' Equity: Common Stock Retained Earnings	$ 10,000 $727,500	$ 10,000 $852,500	$ 10,000 $984,500	$ 10,000 $1,213,500	$ 10,000 $1,547,500
Total Stockholders' Equity	$737,500	$862,500	$994,500	$1,223,500	$1,557,500

Table 5.3
Gate City Video Rental: Selected Items from the Income Statement

	1993	1994	1995	1996	1997
Movie Rentals	$2,200,000	$2,376,000	$2,566,000	$2,771,000	$2,993,000
Net Income	$ 138,000	$ 117,000	$ 56,000	($ 14,000)	($ 130,000)

Table 5.4
Gate City Video Rental: Selected Items from the Balance Sheet

	1993	1994	1995	1996	1997
Stockholders' Equity: Common Stock Retained Earnings	$ 10,000 $102,500	$ 10,000 $219,500	$ 10,000 $275,500	$ 10,000 $261,500	$ 10,000 $131,500
Total Stockholders' Equity	$112,500	$229,500	$285,500	$271,500	$141,500

Table 5.5
Gate City Orthopedic Clinic: Selected Items from the Income Statement

	1993	1994	1995	1996	1997
Patient Revenues	$1,700,000	$1,836,000	$1,983,000	$2,142,000	$2,313,000
Net Income	$ 50,000	$ 75,000	$ 82,000	$ 89,000	$ 97,000

Table 5.6
Gate City Orthopedic Clinic: Selected Items from the Balance Sheet

	1993	1994	1995	1996	1997
Stockholders' Equity: Common Stock Retained Earnings	$ 10,000 $673,500	$ 10,000 $748,500	$ 10,000 $830,500	$ 10,000 $919,500	$ 10,000 $1,016,500
Total Stockholders' Equity	$683,500	$758,500	$840,500	$929,500	$1,026,500

FORECASTING

Recall from Chapter 3 that forecasting is a statistical technique used to extrapolate financial values into the future on the basis of past values. One forecasting method is to fit a linear trend line to existing information. Figure 5.1, Figure 5.2, and Figure 5.3 show the actual net income, in thousands of dollars, from the three businesses over the period 1993 through 1997. Each observed or actual net income value is shown by a "+" mark. Looking at each of the three figures, it is clear, as anticipated from the discussion in Chapter 4 and from an inspection of the net income values in Table 5.1, Table 5.3, and Table 5.5, that there was an upward trend in net income over the years 1993 through 1997 for both Gate City Widget Company and for Gate City Orthopedic Clinic. Also, as expected, the trend in net income for Gate City Video Rental was downward over this period of time.

Imposed on each of these three figures there is a vertical dotted line referenced at the year 1998 to emphasize that pre-1998 observations are actual net income data, and 1998 through 2002 observations are the net income forecasts.

There are several important points to note about the trend line in each figure. First, as in Chapter 3 with reference to Figure 3.1, the line was statistically determined using least-squares regression analysis. As such, it is the best linear representation of the five years of net income data—1993 through 1997. As would be expected, there are actual 1993 through 1997 data points above and below the 1993 through 1997 segment of this line. The least-squares regression line is the best linear approximation of the actual 1993 through 1997 data, and hence, it is not expected to connect each observation over those five years.

Figure 5.1
Gate City Widget Company: Trends in Net Income

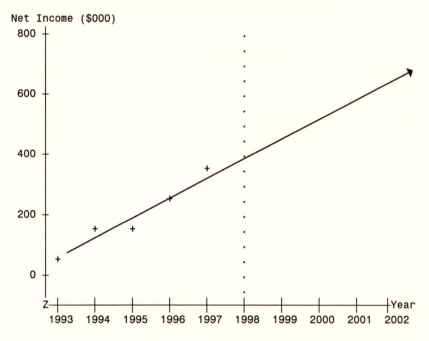

Net Income ($000)

Second, each of the three least-squares regression line equations is presented in Table 5.7 (without derivation). Given these equations, one can simply insert a value for the year to be forecast and calculate the corresponding forecast of net income. The net income forecasts for each of the three businesses are also reported in Table 5.7.

The forecast of net income for each of these businesses is revealing, and by itself it provides useful information for a potential seller as well as for a potential buyer. For the seller, this information provides the quantitative validation of a trend that had likely already been recognized or anticipated from knowledge about the company as well as from a visual inspection of the income statements. For the buyer, it provides quantitative information about the magnitude of future events, assuming that nothing else changes, as well as information relevant to an initial negotiating position.

Keep in mind that there is asymmetry in information regarding the business being valued if it is being valued to be sold, or if the value is to be transferred to another party. Assuming that the financial statements are accurate and that they fully disclose all relevant financial facts, the seller will generally have more information about the economic factors that underlie the trends in the financial data than will the buyer. In general, the seller will, through experience, be able to determine if these relevant economic factors are permanent or transitory. It is incumbent upon the buyer to first identify trends and then delve into the economic factors that caused them, and then into the permanency of these factors. Determining trend is a science; understanding trend is an art.

Figure 5.2
Gate City Video Rental: Trends in Net Income

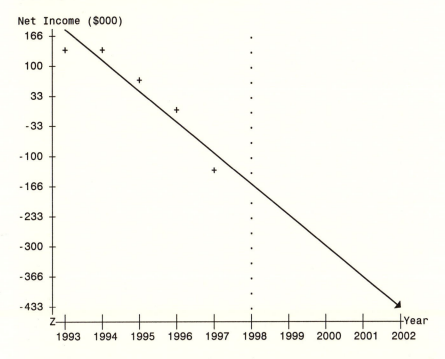

If the valuation is not being conducted for transactions purposes, these trends clearly demonstrate to the audience for the valuation—which could be the Internal Revenue Service if the valuation is being conducted for tax-related matters, or it could be a judge if the valuation is being conducted for equitable distribution purposes—what the future may have in store.

There is an expression that political consultants and lobbyists in Washington, D.C., often use when describing the presentation style they employ when offering information to Congress or to similar political bodies—"dumb it down, and color it up." This descriptor is not intended to disparage either consultants or political groups, rather it is intended to emphasize that these groups are exposed to so much information in such short periods of time that only the essence of additional new information can readily be absorbed, and the essence must make intuitive sense. Our point is that a simple trend line of net income or profits is a common-sense way to initially approach how one thinks about the value of a business, and its trend makes a powerful initial impression. Thus, if the trend is an accurate representation of the future value of the business, then all the better; if it is not, one must understand why.

Figure 5.3
Gate City Orthopedic Clinic: Trends in Net Income

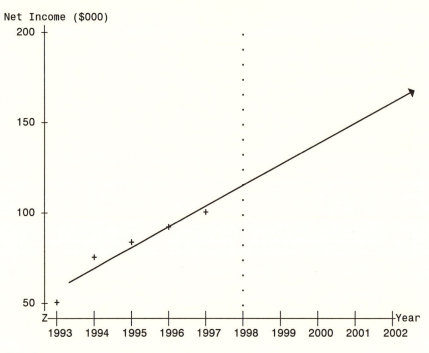

Net Income ($000)

For completeness, we present the estimating equations for the least-squares forecasts of sales and revenues in Table 5.8, and we present in Table 5.9 the estimating equations for the least-squares forecasts of stockholder equity.

It is interesting to compare, for example, the information in Table 5.7 to that in Table 5.8 for Gate City Video Rental. In Table 5.7 it is clear that Gate City Video Rental is forecast to continue to lose money, that is, net income is forecast to decline. Although, as seen in Table 5.8 from the positive coefficient on the variable Year, revenues from video rentals are forecast to grow. Is this inconsistent? No. Keep in mind several points. First, forecasts are linear extrapolations of actual previous financial events. Given that Gate City Video Rental's net income fell over the 1993 through 1997 period, it must be the case that any statistical forecast of future net income will mirror that declining trend. Second, net income is the difference between revenues and operating expenses. An upward trend in revenues does not by itself imply an upward trend in profitability; the latter depends on what operating expenses have done. In the case of Gate City Video Rental, operating expenses have been increasing at a faster rate than have revenues, thus bringing about the decreasing trend in net income.

We reemphasize that forecasts generated solely by regression analysis do not take into account changes in the business's operating environment. For example, what owner or manager faced with the challenges of Gate City Video

Rental would sit idly by and watch losses mount? We cannot think of any such owner or manager. Accordingly, it is reasonable to expect the internal operating environment of Gate City Video Rental to change in the future compared to what he was doing during the 1993 through 1997 period.

We mentioned in Chapter 3 that an alternative to trend line forecasts is to average previous percentage increases and extrapolate from those percentages. The results from this technique are comparable to the results from a trend line forecast, but not identical. Table 5.10 illustrates this using the stockholders' equity data for Gate City Orthopedic Clinic.

Table 5.7
Estimated Equations for Forecasting Net Income and the Forecast of Net Income

---

Gate City Widget Company
    Net Income = -135,087,600 + 67,800 × Year
        1998 forecast: $376,800
        1999 forecast: $444,600
        2000 forecast: $512,400
        2001 forecast: $580,200
        2002 forecast: $648,000
Gate City Video Rental
    Net Income = 133,099,900 - 66,700 × Year
        1998 forecast: -$166,700
        1999 forecast: -$233,400
        2000 forecast: -$300,100
        2001 forecast: -$366,800
        2002 forecast: -$433,500
Gate City Orthopedic Clinic
    Net Income = -21,467,400 + 10,800 × Year
        1998 forecast: $111,000
        1999 forecast: $121,800
        2000 forecast: $132,600
        2001 forecast: $143,400
        2002 forecast: $154,200

Table 5.8
Estimated Equations for Forecasting Sales and Revenues

Gate City Widget Company
    Sales = -701,539,300 + 353,100 × Year
Gate City Video Rental
    Video Rentals = -392,628,300 + 198,100 × Year
Gate City Orthopedic Clinic
    Patient Revenues = -303,639,200 + 153,200 × Year

Table 5.9
Estimated Equations for Forecasting Stockholders' Equity

Gate City Widget Company
    Stockholders' Equity = -398,124,400 + 200,100 × Year
Gate City Video Rental
    Stockholders' Equity = -19,741,900 + 10,000 × Year
Gate City Orthopedic Clinic
    Stockholders' Equity = -170,123,800 + 85,700 × Year

As seen in Table 5.10, the average of the four annual percentage increases (rounded) in stockholders' equity is 10.7 percent. This average annual percentage increase of 10.7 percent is an unweighted average, that is, each of the four percentages is added together and the sum is divided by four. Looking at the four percentages, however, it is clear that the annual percentage increase has declined in each year. Such a decline is normal for a company experiencing rapid growth since constant growth in terms of dollars will necessarily result in declining growth percentages. Perhaps a weighted average of the four percentages would be a more accurate descriptor of future years' activities? The use of a weighted average would explicitly assume that the latter year's growth is more representative of the future than the lack of growth in the former years.

In the lower portion of Table 5.10 we forecast 1998 through 2002 stockholders' equity assuming that 1997 stockholders' equity increases in the future at an annual rate of growth of 10.7 percent. The so-calculated forecasts are shown. Comparing these percentage growth forecasts to the regression line forecasts based on the regression equation in Table 5.9, it is clear that each of the percentage growth forecasts in Table 5.10 is larger. One might logically ask, Which forecast is correct? Both forecasts are correct from a mathematical perspective. The more perceptive question is, Which forecast—regression line forecast or percentage growth forecast—is based on the more realistic set of assumptions? The assumptions underlying the regression line forecasts are:

1. Stockholders' equity between 1993 and 1997 is an accurate predictor of stockholders' equity in future years, with each year being given equal weight.
2. Stockholders' equity in future years will grow in the same linear manner as it grew over the 1993 through 1997 period.

The assumptions underlying the percentage growth forecasts are:

1. 1997 stockholders' equity is an accurate predictor of stockholders' equity in future years.
2. 1997 stockholder's equity will increase in future years at the same average percentage rate that it increased over the 1993 through 1997 period, with each year's percentage being given equal weight.

Table 5.10
Actual and Percentage Growth Forecasts of Stockholders' Equity for Gate City Orthopedic Clinic

Year	Stockholders' Equity	Annual Percentage Change (rounded)
1993	$ 683,500	
		11.0%
1994	$ 758,500	
		10.8%
1995	$ 840,500	
		10.6%
1996	$ 929,500	
		10.4%
1997	$1,026,500	
	Average of Annual Percentages	10.7%

Year	Forecasts Based on 10.7% Growth
1998	$1,136,336
1999	$1,257,924
2000	$1,392,522
2001	$1,541,522
2002	$1,706,465

Year	Regression Line Forecast (from Table 5.9)
1998	$1,104,800
1999	$1,190,500
2000	$1,276,200
2001	$1,361,900
2002	$1,447,600

There are subtle differences in these assumptions. The most important difference is that the regression line forecast assumes linearity based on the linear pattern from 1993 through 1997. That is, as we discussed in Chapter 2, the regression line forecast is based on the forecast of the 1997 value. In contrast, the percentage growth forecast is based on the actual value for 1997.

We have seen business valuators use regression line forecasts, and we have seen business valuators use percentage growth forecasts, although only one method is generally used throughout a particular business valuation. We do not offer here a blanket statement that one forecasting method is always preferred over another, or over other methods not discussed in this book. Rather, we emphasize the importance of understanding the subtle difference in the assumptions that underlie the methods considered before selecting a particular method.

It is our general practice to fit a regression line to the data at hand and from it to examine the strength of the assumption of linearity. But, we do not stop there. Our next step is to relate the economic environment of the business in the past to the economic environment that will likely exist in the future. When they are the same, and if the data do support the assumption of linearity, then we may likely proceed with regression line forecasts. When they are not the same, then our choice of a forecast is guided by the economic environment that will likely exist in the future.

WEIGHTED AVERAGES

As will become evident in the application of alternative valuation methods to the three businesses being discussed, weighted averages of financial data are fundamental to many of the standard valuation methods. Recall from Chapter 3 that a weighted average is simply a numerical average of numbers where each number is weighted in a manner that is assumed to reflect its relevance to future activity. Therein we discussed the typical 5-4-3-2-1 weighting scheme and illustrated it using hypothetical data.

Table 5.11 shows the weighted average of previous sales and revenues, of previous net income, and of previous stockholders' equity based on the financial data for each business for the 1993 through 1997 period.

Table 5.11
Weighted Average (5-4-3-2-1) of Relevant Financial Data

Gate City Widget Company	
Weighted average of sales	$3,130,600
Weighted average of net income	$ 218,600
Weighted average of stockholders' equity	$1,208,500
Gate City Video Rental	
Weighted average of video rentals	$2,713,267
Weighted average of net income	$ -11,067
Weighted average of stockholders' equity	$ 214,767
Gate City Orthopedic Clinic	
Weighted average of patient revenues	$2,096,933
Weighted average of net income	$ 85,800
Weighted average of stockholders' equity	$ 904,833

Mathematically, a weighted average of previous year's data must be a smaller value than the current year's value if there has been growth. As such, a weighted average serves as a descriptor of previous activity with emphasis on the more recent year. Looking at the weighted averages in Table 5.11 in isolation from the other forecast information in other tables tells one little about the future of the businesses. It is simply a mathematically derived number that is fundamental to many valuation methods. We will illustrate this point in detail in later chapters.

6

DISCOUNT RATES AND CAPITALIZATION RATES

Great deeds are usually wrought at great risks.
—Herodotus

INTRODUCTION

In our discussion in Chapter 2 regarding the purpose of a business, we asked the following question, How much money must a business make to continue to operate? We then answered the question by stating that it is reasonable to expect that the owner of a business will continue to operate the business as long as the business generates or is expected to generate a return greater than the return the owner could earn in a comparable alternative investment. We went on to explain this rather common-sense statement using more formal economic terminology, namely, the owner will continue to operate the business as long as the business earns above the opportunity cost of the invested resources in the business.

To relate this concept of the opportunity cost of the resources invested in the business to the value of the business, we introduced in Chapter 3 the concept of present value and referred to it as a basic valuation tool. Recall that we defined present value, PV, in terms of the value today of an asset with a known value in the future. If the asset has a known value of \$X one year in the future, then the value of that asset today—its present value—can be determined as:

$$PV = \$X/(1 + r)^1 \tag{6.1}$$

where r represents the discount rate or the alternative annual rate of return. This formula was previously presented in Chapter 3 as equation (3.4), and there we described the discount rate, r, as the rate that could be earned on a comparable alternative investment.

More generally, the present value of n annual series of equal future assets with known values is:

$$PV = [\$X/(1 + r)^1] + [\$X/(1 + r)^2] + \ldots + [\$X/(1 + r)^n] \qquad (6.2)$$

or, using general notation:

$$PV = \$X \{[(1 + r)^n - 1]/[r(1 + r)^n]\} \qquad (6.3)$$

Equation (6.3) is a generalization of equation (6.2). For n very large, that is, as n approaches ∞, r is referred to as the capitalization rate. In such a case:

$$PV = \$X/r \qquad (6.4)$$

To reemphasize, the science of present value calculations as defined by equation (6.3) is simple. The art of present value calculations involves, among other things, estimating a value for a comparable alternative investment, r.

The purpose of this chapter is to discuss in detail present value calculations by discussing the art of how to estimate a value of r.

RETURN ON INVESTMENT

The return that can be earned on certain investments can be known with 100 percent certainty, and the return that can be earned on other investments can be known with a probability that is less than 100 percent. Those investments for which there is less than a 100 percent probability of knowing the exact return that will be earned are said to be investments that are characterized by risk.

Risk is defined as the probability that the actual return on an investment will differ from its expected return. Risk is not good or bad; risk is only a characterization of the likelihood that expectations will be realized. In that sense risk is an aspect of reality, and it is important that all business valuations conform as closely to reality as possible.

From a statistical perspective, risk can be measured in probability terms. From an ex post point of view, if an individual invests $100 with the expectation of earning 10 percent over the next year, but at the end of the year realizes something other than a 10 percent rate of return, then the investment is said to have been risky. From an ex ante, point of view, if the individual invests $100 but thinks that there is a 70 percent probability that the investment will earn 10 percent, a 20 percent probability that the investment will earn 9 percent, and a 10 percent probability that the investment will earn 11 percent, then the investment is likewise said to be risky because the actual return is likely to differ from the expected return. In this particular example, the investor could calculate a probability weighted return, or an expected return assuming that the ex ante probabilities are in fact known and are correct.

As a semantic aside, risk is not the same as uncertainty. Uncertainty characterizes an investment choice for which the investor has no information about the return to be earned on the investment, whereas with risk an estimate can be made about the probabilities associated with the alternative returns.

It is a well-documented fact that individuals are willing to accept greater risk in an investment only if there is also a greater expected return. This so-called risk-return tradeoff makes perfect sense. Why would an individual subject an investment to greater risk without the expectation of greater return?

Figure 6.1 illustrates the risk-return tradeoff for a risk neutral individual. The tradeoff line is drawn linearly. If there is an increase in risk in the amount shown by the shift ($\rightarrow$) of the vertical dotted lines along the horizontal axis, this risk neutral investor will need to be compensated by an equal return as shown along the vertical axis. Figure 6.2 illustrates the risk-return tradeoff for a risk averse individual. This illustrated individual will require a greater return than the risk neutral individual to accept the same increase in risk. Finally, Figure 6.3 illustrates the risk-return tradeoff for a risk taking individual. In this case, a small additional return is needed for this individual to accept the increase in risk. Our point in making these conceptual, illustration-based distinctions is to emphasize that risk, as applied to business valuations, is a subjective concept because all investors will vary in their proclivity for taking risk. If individuals differ in their proclivity for taking risk, they will also differ in their perception of comparable alternative investments. It is quite likely that buyers and sellers will so differ.

Figure 6.1
The Risk-Return Tradeoff: A Risk Neutral Individual

Return

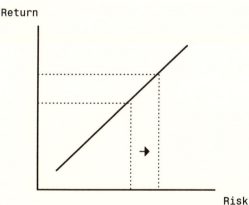

Risk

Consider a business that is expected to earn a net income of $100,000 in each of the next five years. Assume that the present value of this stream of net income is a reasonable first approximation of the fair market value of the business, then the calculation of the fair market value of the business rests entirely on the choice of the discount rate. The choice of a higher discount rate will produce a lower present value estimate; the choice of a lower discount rate will produce a higher present value estimate. From the seller's perspective, through experience there is an accumulation of knowledge about the inherent risk associated with operating the business. The seller, if objective, can identify in general terms other businesses of comparable risk. For illustrative purposes, assume that the seller could view an investment from which one would earn a 15 percent rate of return with certainty as a comparable alternative to the risk involved in owning and operating the business. Thus, the seller would approximate the value of the business using a 15 percent discount rate as:

$$
\begin{aligned}
\text{Seller's Value of the Business} &= \$100{,}000/(1.15)^1 + \$100{,}000/(1.15)^2 + \\
&\quad \$100{,}000/(1.15)^3 + \$100{,}000/(1.15)^4 + \\
&\quad \$100{,}000/(1.15)^5 \\
&= \$335{,}216 \quad\quad\quad\quad\quad\quad (6.5)
\end{aligned}
$$

Figure 6.2
The Risk-Return Tradeoff: A Risk Averse Individual

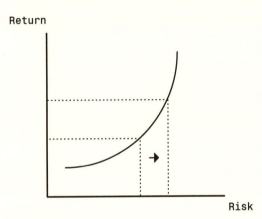

Figure 6.3
The Risk-Return Tradeoff: A Risk Taking Individual

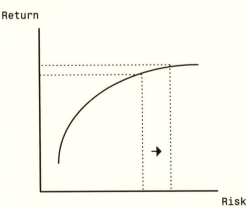

From the buyer's perspective, risk may be viewed differently. Assume the buyer views the fact that the seller has only one major customer who accounts for 80 percent of revenues and that the seller has no long-term contract between the two as a substantial element of risk. The seller, however, may not view this as an element of risk because of a longstanding personal relationship with the owner of the other business. In contrast, the seller may view the company's high turnover rate of its assembly line workers as a significant element of risk; the buyer may not view this as an important element of risk because of what he or she believes is superior management ability.

If, in the buyer's opinion, these factors net to the expectation of a 20 percent return being the return that could be earned on a comparable alternative investment, then the buyer will approximate the value of the business as:

$$\text{Buyer's Value of the Business} = \$100,000/(1.20)^1 + \$100,000/(1.20)^2 + \$100,000/(1.20)^3 + \$100,000/(1.20)^4 + \$100,000/(1.20)^5$$
$$= \$299,061 \tag{6.6}$$

Or, if the buyer perceives a 10 percent return on a comparable alternative investment, then the buyer will approximate the value of the business as:

$$\text{Buyer's Value of the Business} = \$100,000/(1.10)^1 + \$100,000/(1.10)^2 + \$100,000/(1.10)^3 + \$100,000/(1.10)^4 + \$100,000/(1.10)^5$$
$$= \$379,079 \tag{6.7}$$

Financial incentives aside, it is reasonable to expect that a buyer and a seller will have different initial opinions about the value of a business even though both are looking at the same financial information. These differences are due, in large part, to perceptions about the risk of the business. As illustrated in Figures 6.1 through 6.3, differences in perception of risk are in part a reflection of the innate tendencies of the individuals toward risk in general.

SYSTEMATIC APPROACHES TO APPROXIMATING RISK

Risk characterizes all business activities, but it is not a characteristic that can easily be quantified. Risk is a subjective characterization of a business and its economic environment. While most business valuators realize this, there are those who will attempt to avoid subjectivity in a valuation exercise, that is, there are those who will avoid the art of business valuation and attempt to make all aspects of valuation a science. Such individuals typically rely on others' quantitative generalizations about risk and impose others' generalizations on the valuation exercise in an attempt to make it appear more objective than it really is. We understand why this is done, but we eschew the practice.

Excellent research however has been done by many scholars in an effort to approximate risk. For example, Ralph Badger in his 1925 book, *Valuation of*

Industrial Securities, generalized that business activities fall broadly into one of four categories: low risk, medium risk, high risk, and very high risk. For each class, based on his analysis of industrial securities, he estimated the rate of return that investors would require (investors are a proxy for buyers of a closely held company). For example, investors at that time (1925) would require between 12 percent and 14.99 percent to invest in a low-risk business; they would in contrast require over a 25 percent return to invest in a very high-risk business. But, who is to say objectively what a low risk business is? Company A could be, in one valuator's mind, toward the upper end of the distribution of low-risk businesses; or it could be in the second valuator's mind, toward the lower end of the distribution of medium-risk businesses.

In *The Financial Policy of Corporations* (1953), Arthur Dewing generalized about the relationship between the organizational structure of a business and its risk (and hence the return an investor would require to invest in the business). His organizational taxonomy has seven categories ranging from an old established business with large capital assets and excellent goodwill for which an investor would require a low rate of return such as 10 percent, to a personal service business for which the earnings of the enterprise are the objective reflection of the owner's skills for which an investor would require a very high rate of return such as 100 percent. Again, while Dewing provides carefully derived percentages, subjectivity remains in using these percentages since Company A must still be placed uniquely in one category or another.

One of the most frequently cited studies on risk quantifications was conducted by James Schilt. His article, "A Rational Approach to Capitalization Rates for Discounting the Future Income Stream of a Closely Held Company," appeared in *The Financial Planner* in 1982. Schilt's premise was that general guidelines associated with the quantification of risk would be useful to those involved in discounting or capitalizing streams of future assets.

Before discussing Schilt's findings, it is useful to put his research into a broader context. The return required by an investor is comprised of three parts. The first part is an estimate of the expected rate of inflation, the second part is what economists call the real rate of interest or the finite return to an investor for sacrificing current purchasing opportunities for future purchasing opportunities, and the third part is a premium for accepting the risk that characterizes the investment. Thus, the investor's required return on investment (ROI) is:

$$
\begin{aligned}
\text{ROI} = {}& \text{compensation for inflation} + \\
& \text{compensation for foregone purchasing opportunities} + \\
& \text{compensation for risk} \\
= {}& \text{expected rate of inflation} + \\
& \text{real rate of interest} + \\
& \text{risk premium}
\end{aligned}
\tag{6.8}
$$

An investor will, at a minimum, want to be compensated for what is called the time value of money. This means that due to inflation, \$1 one year from now will have less purchasing power than \$1 has today, so it will be of lesser value.

As prices increase over a year, the purchasing power of $1 declines. For an investor to invest in a business, and thereby relinquish the purchasing power of $1 now, the investor will, at a minimum, expect to be compensated for decreases in the purchasing power of $1 over the course of the investment. A reasonable approximation of the decrease in the purchasing power of money is the expected rate of inflation.

Economists estimate that the real rate of interest, or the cost to an investor for sacrificing current purchasing opportunities for future purchasing opportunities, holding inflation constant, is constant at about 2.5 percent to 3 percent per year. We accept this premise, and we will return to it below.

An investor, in addition to being compensated for inflation and for foregone purchasing opportunities, will also want to be compensated for the pure risk associated with the investment. The greater such perceived risk, the greater the return that the investor will require. It is this risk premium that Schilt considered in his research. As shown in Table 6.1, Schilt devised five categories of risk and described, in the most general of terms, the operational characteristics of businesses that are likely to fall into each category. As seen in Table 6.1, well-established businesses with a depth of management are less risky than small proprietorships. Albeit the Schilt scheme is frequently used by valuators despite the fact that the scheme has no methodological foundation, subjectivity still remains as to which risk category most appropriately represents the business in question.

Finally, the most systematically collected and analyzed data on risk premiums are those prepared by R. G. Ibbotson Associates, as reported in the most recent edition of *Stocks, Bonds, Bills, and Inflation.* Ibbotson and his associates relied on market data rather than on the operational characteristics of businesses to arrive at the numerical value of risk factors. These factors are based on percentage of earnings by publicly traded companies above a risk-free rate of return, such as that earned on a U.S. Treasury bond. For example, one can conclude from the Ibbotson data that the market places a higher return on small companies than on large, and from that observed fact one can infer that small companies are generally more risky. This conclusion is not inconsistent with the observations by Schilt or even by Dewing, and its use in a particular valuation is subject to the same cautions that we addressed above.

It is more common than not, at least based on our experience, for a business valuator to approximate a discount rate or capitalization rate by going through steps similar to the following:

Step 1: Posit that the expected rate of inflation plus the real rate of interest can be estimated in terms of a risk-free rate of return on a long-term U.S. Treasury bond.
Step 2: Examine the management and organizational structure of the business being valued, place it in one of Schilt's five categories (or similar published categories), and then assume that the relevant risk premium to be added to the risk-free rate of return from Step 1 is within Schilt's suggested range of values.
Step 3: Conclude that the determination of the discount rate or capitalization rate was objective, relying on published government statistics on Treasury bond yields and on Schilt's long-standing research.

These steps do give the appearance of a systematic and objective approach to determining a discount rate or capitalization rate. However, the placement of the business being valued into one of Schilt's arbitrary categories is extremely subjective, and that fact poses problems with this method.

Table 6.1
Categories of Risk and Associated Business Characteristics

Risk Category	Characteristics of Business	Risk Premium
1	Established businesses with a strong trade position, are well financed, have depth in management, whose past earnings have been stable and whose future is highly predictable.	6-10%
2	Established businesses in a more competitive industry that are well financed, have depth of management, have stable past earnings and whose future is fairly predictable.	11-15%
3	Businesses in a highly competitive industry that require little capital to enter, no management depth, element of risk is high, although past record may be good.	16-20%
4	Small businesses that depend upon the special skill of one or two people. Larger established businesses that are highly cyclical in nature. In both cases, future earnings may be expected to deviate widely from projections.	21-25%
5	Small "one man" businesses of a personal services nature, where the transferability of the income stream is in question.	26-30%

Source: James H. Schilt, "A Rational Approach to Capitalization Rates for Discounting the Future Income Stream of a Closely Held Company," *The Financial Planner,* January 1982, p. 58.

We prefer a more forthright approach, one that states up front that there are subjective aspects to any business valuation, the most common aspect of which is the determination of a discount rate or capitalization rate. No apology for this fact is needed. We prefer a build-up method.

BUILD-UP METHOD FOR DETERMINING DISCOUNT RATES AND CAPITALIZATION RATES

We prefer to build a discount rate or a capitalization rate, starting with the elements that an investor—buyer or seller—will require in terms of a return on investment and adding numerical estimates of those values to a risk-free rate of return. This concept of building a discount rate or a capitalization rate is certainly not unique to us. Authors advocate such a practice, and many valuators employ such a concept. While there is precedent for this approach, it must be emphasized that this approach is not scientific. Regardless of the sophistication that one brings to the build-up method, it is replete with subjective judgment about the exact values to impute to each element. Again, subjectivity cannot be avoided in a business valuation. We believe that it is the business valuator's responsibility to be forthright about which aspects of the valuation are subjective and the reasoning that is behind each subjectively determined value. It should not be the business valuator's goal to avoid subjectivity at any cost. Business valuation is part art, and the art of business valuation rests on subjective concepts.

To elaborate again on this last theme, the reader of this book should not infer that the business valuator who writes in the most eloquent fashion or who is a gifted orator is the most "artistic." It may be the case that such a valuator carries the day in a court of law, but our intent in this book is not to explain advocacy. Rather, it is to describe what we believe, based quite frankly from an evolutionary process, is the correct process to business valuation and not to focus on a means to achieve a particular partisan goal.

The build-up method for determining the return that a seller will require from the assets received from the sale of a business, or the return that a buyer will require from the purchase of the business, is what we have abbreviated as ROI—return on investment. As we have previously stated, it is this comparable alternative return that is the conceptually correct interpretation of a discount rate or capitalization rate.

As shown in equation (6.8), there are three parts of ROI: the expected rate of inflation, the real rate of interest, and the risk premium that describes the business or its comparable alternative investment. The first two parts of ROI taken together are appropriately approximated by the return on a risk-free asset. The risk-free rate of return is correctly approximated by the yield on a long-term Treasury bond.

Corporate bonds are not a risk-free investment. While the yield is stated on a corporate bond, its price is subject to market fluctuations and hence the actual return earned on a corporate bond is variable. Thus, yields on corporate bonds are an inappropriate proxy to use for these two elements of equation (6.8).

Treasury securities are risk free in the sense that there is approximately zero probability of default and approximately zero probability of earning a return other than that stated on the security. The return on a thirty-year Treasury bond is generally considered the most appropriate long-term risk-free return. However, if the investor's time horizon is shorter than thirty years, then the yield on a shorter-term bond could be the more appropriate rate to use. For example, an investor may consider purchasing Company A with the intention of operating the business for ten years and then retiring. This potential buyer could correctly evaluate the risk-free opportunity cost in terms of a ten-year Treasury bond. The same applies to the seller's evaluation of the horizon for his or her comparable alternative investment.

Yields on Treasury securities are published daily in the *Wall Street Journal*, in other financial newspapers, and in many national and local newspapers. Also, daily yields are readily available from security brokers and are public through electronic media.

As discussed in the previous section of this chapter, some writers have set forth qualitative and quantitative guidelines for estimating the risk premium. Our version of the build-up method is more appropriate than adherence to some quantitative template. The elements of the build-up method relate to the general economic environment in which the business operates and is expected to operate in the future, and the ability of the potential buyer to replicate the management capabilities of the existing owner of the business. The steps we follow when building a discount rate or a capitalization rate are annotated in Table 6.2. One begins with the risk-free rate of return and then increases that percentage to account for:

- competitive risk,
- regulatory risk,
- cost risk,
- customer risk,
- marketability risk, and
- financial risk.

The order in which these elements of risk are considered is not relevant. Explicit in the table is the absence of quantitative measures to associate with each risk category. While it would be nice to offer such a template, not only would one be so general as not to be applicable in any particular situation, but it would also invite misuse.

A business valuator must consider each of these six aspects of risk and make a judgment on how relevant they are to the business being valued, and if relevant, then how much they influence the value of the discount rate or capitalization rate. There are some very limited market indicators that could be helpful in this task. For example, it is generally the case that the rate charged by a financial institution for a fifteen-year or thirty-year mortgage is greater than the risk-free fifteen-year or thirty-year Treasury bond rate, respectively. The reason for this is that the probability of default on a Treasury bond is zero, whereas the probability of default on a mortgage is greater than zero and variable across borrowers. Such differences in rates provide some indication of how the market views the risk of default. It is hard to imagine a business with less risk than this market-determined risk of default. Also, there are published aggregate financial statistics, by industry, that one can use to compare to the business being valued to gain some insight into the financial risk that may characterize the business.

Beyond these two guidelines, it is our opinion that quantifying the additional elements in the build-up method will require the informed judgment of the valuator. Insights offered by the seller of the business can also be helpful, as can insights from owners of comparable businesses.

It is an art to understand in detail each of the six risk categories in such detail so as to describe them objectively to whomever the audience for the valuation is. To then translate that art into numbers for use in relevant valuation formulae is subjective and will, in all likelihood, be the single most contemplated aspect of a valuation. The extent to which two valuators differ in this dimensions is, in part, based on their ability to understand the elements of risk and on their objectivity in describing and then quantifying them.

Table 6.2
Build-Up Method for Determining Discount Rates and Capitalization Rates

Steps in the Build-Up Method	Comments
Step 1 Begin with the risk-free rate of return, then add to the risk-free rate percentage points that reflect aspects of risk.	Estimation of the risk-free rate of return comes from the yield on a long-term Treasury bond. Select the term to maturity of the bond to correspond to the investor's time horizon for the investment.
Step 2 Consider adding percentage points based on the competitive environment of the business.	Competitive risk includes (i) relevant trends in the industry or economy, or (ii) if the number of domestic or international competitors is large and if they are expected to increase, or (iii) if the technology that underlies the provision of the good or service is expected to change thus making the good or service technologically obsolete, or (iv) company specific factors such as management depth, name recognition, financial stability, or product diversity.
Step 3 Consider adding percentage points based on the regulatory environment of the business.	Regulatory risk increases (i) if there are existing federal or state regulations that affect the provision of the good or service and if they are expected to increase, or (ii) if new regulations are expected to be enacted.

(Table 6.2 continued)

Steps in the Build-Up Method	Comments
Step 4 Consider adding percentage points based on the cost environment of the business.	Cost risk increases (i) if the business relies on only one supplier for any critical manufacturing materials or resources, or (ii) if the industry of suppliers is expected to become less competitive, or (iii) if critical manufacturing materials or resources are in limited supply.
Step 5 Consider adding percentage points based on the character of the customer base.	Customer risk increases if revenues are skewed toward only a few customers and if there are no transferable long-term contractual agreements.
Step 6 Consider adding percentage points based on the nonmarketability of revenue-generating assets.	Marketability risk increases (i) if critical operations rely on only a few key individuals, or (ii) if revenues are tied to nontransferable intellectual property (e.g., patents or licenses).
Step 7 Consider adding percentage points based on long-term financial obligations, then add all elements together.	Financial risk increases if long-term obligations will impede long-term growth.

7

COMPARABILITY

Comparisons are odious.
—Fortescue

INTRODUCTION

An important conclusion from our previous discussions about the economic environment of a business is that economic environments differ from business to business, and the economic environment of a particular business changes over time. Every business is unique in terms of its management, and many businesses are unique in terms of the goods and services that they produce (substitutes exist for most goods and services). Although the economic environment of a business is what it is, the uniqueness of a business's management and products makes the influence of the economic environment on business activity unique in its own right. Thus, one might reasonably question the logic of including in this book this chapter on comparability.

Our purpose in this chapter is not to suggest that one can determine the value of a business precisely from the value of comparable businesses. Rather, our purpose is to summarize the insights that one can gain from examining how closely or not the business being valued compares in the most general financial terms to other businesses. Comparability is one of many pieces of information that a valuator brings to the valuation exercise. As with most nonspecific pieces of information, care must be exercised in how such information is interpreted and utilized in arriving at the final valuation opinion. That said, we believe that the best indicator of a business's value is based on the value of a truly identical comparable business. However, it is our experience that truly identical companies rarely exist.

ASPECTS OF COMPARABILITY

What should be compared? We will discuss in later chapters situations in which the sales price of comparable companies is useful information in a valuation exercise. In this chapter, however, we examine financial statistics that can shed some light on the extent to which the to-be-valued business is like other businesses in what could be considered the same broadly defined industry. The usefulness of these comparisons is primarily to assist the valuator in determining the aspects of risk that characterize the business.

Recall from Chapter 6 that the build-up method for determining the discount rate and the capitalization rate requires the valuator to consider a number of risk-related aspects of the business. These risk-related aspects of the business include competitive risk, regulatory risk, cost risk, customer risk, marketability risk, and financial risk. Through comparisons with other similar businesses—and similar is a somewhat subjective term, as we discussed in Chapter 2—the valuator can gain insights into at least the financial risk of the business. These insights regarding financial risk are important reflections of the manner in which the existing management has operated the company. How the existing management has operated the company may influence how a potential buyer perceives the ability to deviate in the future from the company's historical record on profitability.

RATIO ANALYSIS

A ratio is an expression of a mathematical relationship between one quantity and another. Ratio analysis can disclose relationships that reveal conditions and trends that often cannot be easily noticed from an inspection of the individual components of a financial statement. Ratios are generally not significant in themselves, but they assume significance when they are compared with previous ratios for the business, ratios of other businesses in the same industry, and industrywide ratios.

One of a number of possible taxonomies for considering financial ratios is to categorize them into the following three groups:

- liquidity ratios,
- capital structure ratios, and
- profitability ratios.

Liquidity ratios reflect the ability of the business to meet its current financial obligations, as summarized in Table 7.1; capital structure ratios reflect the long-term solvency of the business, as summarized in Table 7.2; and profitability ratios reflect the extent to which the business is operated in a profitable manner, as summarized in Table 7.3.

Many valuators rely on the *Annual Statement Studies* published by Robert Morris Associates (RMA) for comparable ratios. This publication contains detailed information on many of the ratios described in Table 7.1, Table 7.2, and Table 7.3 for very broadly defined industries. Care must be exercised, as we have noted above, when using this or any other source of information on comparable statistics. It is science to understand how to calculate a financial ratio; it is art to know how to use and how not to use a financial ratio.

Table 7.1
Liquidity Ratios

Liquidity Ratio	Formula	Interpretation
Current (or working)	$\dfrac{\text{current assets}}{\text{current liabilities}}$	General test of short-term debt-paying ability
Acid-test (or quick)	$\dfrac{\text{securities + receivables}}{\text{current liabilities}}$	More severe test of short-term debt-paying ability
Cash	$\dfrac{\text{cash}}{\text{current liabilities}}$	Most severe test of short-term debt-paying ability
Receivables turnover	$\dfrac{\text{sales (net)}}{\text{average receivables (net)}}$	Efficiency in collecting receivables and in managing credit
Age of receivables	$\dfrac{365}{\text{receivables turnover}}$	Extent of control over credit and collections
Inventory turnover	$\dfrac{\text{cost of goods sold}}{\text{average inventory}}$	Marketability of inventory, efficiency in managing inventory, and reasonableness of quantity of inventory on hand
Days in inventory	$\dfrac{365}{\text{inventory turnover}}$	Average number of days required to sell inventory
Working capital turnover	$\dfrac{\text{sales (net)}}{\text{average working capital}}$	Extent to which working capital is used to generate sales
Number of days' purchases in ending accounts payable	$\dfrac{\text{accounts payable}}{\text{average daily purchases}}$	Extent to which bills are paid promptly

One financial ratio that may be important when valuing a business, and one that is not generally listed with the more traditional financial ratios like those in Table 7.1, Table 7.2, and Table 7.3, is the ratio of officers', directors' and owners' compensation to sales, or the percentage of sales allocated to officers, directors, and owners in the form of compensation. For example, a business may appear to be outstanding in terms of its profitability or net income performance only because the owner of the business is taking a very small portion of revenues in the form of salary or compensation. In such a case, a potential buyer might normalize the business's income statement and impute a more reasonable level of compensation, thus lowering net income and hence the offer price.

Table 7.2
Capital Structure Ratios

Capital Structure Ratio	Formula	Interpretation
Owners' equity to total assets	total owners' equity / total assets (net)	Proportion of assets provided by owners
Owner's equity to total liabilities	total owners' equity / total liabilities	Relative claims of owners and creditors to rest of business
Fixed assets to total equity	total owners' equity / fixed assets (net)	Extent of owners' capital available as working capital
Book value per share of common stock	common stock equity / number of shares of common stock	Financial statement net assets per share of common stock
Total liabilities to total assets	total liabilities / total assets (net)	Protection available to creditors and extent to which business is trading on equity
Total liabilities to owners' equity	total liabilities / owners' equity	Relationship between what is owed to what is owned

The issue of normalizing the income statement to account for a reasonable salary or compensation is not only common when valuing a business for possible sale, but also when valuing a business for equitable distribution purposes. In the latter case, one party in the divorce might argue that the fair market value of the other party's business is too high or too low due to insufficient or excessive compensation. RMA's *Annual Statement Studies* is one source for industry data on the percentage of sales allocated to officers, directors, and owners. Another useful source of such information that relates specifically to the medical profession is the *Physician Compensation and Production Survey* published by the Medical Group Management Association.

Therefore, among the groups of common financial ratios that are summarized in the above three tables, one does not normally see a compensation to sales ratio. However, it is one of the first ratios that we examine when we undertake a valuation.

Table 7.3
Profitability Ratios

Profitability Ratio	Formula	Interpretation
Net income to sales	$$\frac{\text{net income}}{\text{net sales}}$$	Profit margin per dollar of sales
Operation	$$\frac{\text{cost of goods sold + operating expenses}}{\text{net sales}}$$	Profit margin per dollar of sales
Sales to total assets (or asset turnover)	$$\frac{\text{net sales}}{\text{average total assets}}$$	Productivity of assets in generating sales
Earnings per share of common stock	$$\frac{\text{net income - preferred dividend requirements}}{\text{number of shares of common stock}}$$	Return on common stockholders' investment per share of common stock
Price/earnings	$$\frac{\text{market price per share of common stock}}{\text{net income per share of common stock}}$$	Market price for a share of earnings
Dividend yield	$$\frac{\text{cash dividends per share of common stock}}{\text{market price per share of common stock}}$$	Cash yield or return on common stock
Return on assets	$$\frac{\text{net income}}{\text{total assets}}$$	Yield on total assets
Return on common stockholders' equity	$$\frac{\text{net income}}{\text{common stockholders' equity}}$$	Yield on investment to common stockholders
Payout	$$\frac{\text{cash dividends}}{\text{net income}}$$	Extent to which current earnings are distributed to stockholders
Cash flow from operations per share of common stock	$$\frac{\text{net income adjusted for non-cash items}}{\text{number of shares of common stock}}$$	Cash generated per share of common stock from operations of business

COMPARABILITY OF THE THREE BUSINESS EXAMPLES

The three business examples that form the basis for the valuation examples in this book are examined in this chapter in terms of industry ratios. No inferences are drawn from these comparisons except to note how each business compares to the industry average. A valuation error that is often made, especially by those who approach valuation in a mechanical fashion by simply plugging numbers into formulae, is to interpret a reported industry ratio as the norm, or the normal financial behavior within the industry. We cannot emphasize enough that the economic environment of the business being valued influences financial behavior, and any comparison of financial behavior in the absence of a complete understanding of the economic environment, as well as of the competitive strategy adopted by the owner of the business to deal with the economic environment, will in all likelihood result in an inaccurate valuation.

Gate City Widget Company

Table 7.4 compares the financial performance of Gate City Widget Company to its industry, the machine tools and metalworking equipment industry (SIC 3541) in four dimensions. Financial data for 1996 taken from Table 4.1 and Table 4.2 are used to correspond to the most recent data published by RMA. Gate City Widget Company's current ratio is noticeably greater than the industry average, indicating a better-than-average position of liquidity. The company is also earning greater than the industry average of these assets. Its return on assets is 13 percent compared to 7 percent for the industry. The company is also very profitable in dollar terms. Its ratio of net income to sales is nearly 60 percent greater than the industry average; net income for the company is 7 percentage of sales compared to 4.4 percent of sales for the industry. Officers' compensation as a percentage of sales for the industry is 6.9 percent, but Gate City Widget's is 7 percent.

Table 7.4
Comparison of Gate City Widget Company to the Industry, 1996

Financial Ratio	Gate City Widget Company	Industry
Current ratio	2.60	1.80
Net income to sales	0.07	0.044
Return on assets	0.13	0.07
Officers' compensation to sales	0.07	0.069

Source: *Annual Statement Studies, 1997*, Robert Morris Associates, p. 220.

Table 7.5 compares the financial performance of Gate City Video Rental to its industry, video tape rentals (SIC 7841) in the same four dimensions as above. While Gate City Video compares favorably to the industry in terms of its current ratio, the company is losing money, and hence, its net income to sales ratio is negative and its return on investment is a nonexistent datum. Perhaps one reason for its relatively unfavorable financial position is that the officers are drawing a relatively excessive salary, nearly 12 percent of sales compared to only 4.9 percent for the industry.

Table 7.6 compares only Dr. Breslow's salary at Gate City Orthopedic Clinic to the industry, orthopedic surgeons (SIC 8011). Based only on that dimension of comparability, Gate City Orthopedic Clinic's owner's compensation is over 40 percent above the industry norm.

Table 7.5
Comparison of Gate City Video Rental to the Industry, 1996

Financial Ratio	Gate City Video Rental	Industry
Current ratio	0.84	0.9
Net income to sales	-0.005	0.065
Return on investment	not relevant	0.091
Compensation to sales	0.12	0.049

Source: Annual Statement Studies, 1997, Robert Morris Associates, p. 940.

Table 7.6
Comparison of Gate City Orthopedic Clinic to the Industry, 1996

Financial Element	Gate City Orthopedic Clinic	Industry
Compensation per physician	$450,000	$310,475

Note: Compensation refers only to Bruce Breslow.

Source: Physician Compensation and Production Survey: 1997 Report Based on 1996 Data, Medical Group Management Association, p. 26.

Comparisons are indeed odious, but they are an important aspect of business valuations. To return to our previous comparison of appraising a home and valuing a business, one of the first inquiries that an appraiser will make is to determine if comparable homes have been sold, and if yes, the appraiser will use that information to determine the appraisal of the home in question. The same is true for a valuator. One of the first inquires that a valuator will make is to determine if truly identical comparable businesses have been sold, and if yes, then the valuator will use that information to determine a valuation of the business. An important factor that the valuator will use to determine just how comparable other business are to the one in question is the financial ratios discussed in this chapter.

8

ALTERNATIVE VALUATION
METHODS

Circumstances rule men; men do not rule circumstances.
—Herodotus

INTRODUCTION

Four valuation methods are presented in this chapter and each is discussed from a conceptual as well as an implementation perspective. We will illustrate the specific application of each method in Chapters 9, 10, and 11 as related to the three businesses previously discussed. The four methods discussed herein do not represent a complete menu of choices that a valuator will consider. There are several dozen valuation methods discussed throughout the academic and professional literatures, and probably more than that are actually being used within the profession.

The choice of a valuation method requires thought and contemplation. The valuator should first learn about the business and then select the one valuation method that is the "most appropriate" based on the relationship between the circumstances for understanding the valuation and the assumptions that underlie each of the valuation methods. The valuator should not, in our opinion, define "most appropriate" based on the results that follow from the application of several methods. There should be an a priori reason for selecting one valuation method over another.

Recall from Chapter 1 that we emphasized that understanding the appropriateness of one valuation method over another is an aspect of the art of business valuation. The hallmark of a complete valuation is, in our opinion, the objective justification that the valuator gives for the selection of the applied method.

Although our intent in this chapter is neither to review nor belabor previous discussions, one point does warrant repeating. In Chapter 2 we emphasized the underlying assumptions of a business valuation and how those underlying assumptions define the appropriate definition of value to use in a business valuation, namely, fair market value versus liquidation value. We also stated in that chapter that it has been our experience that some business valuators will assume both of these definitions, implement alternative valuation methods, and then average the results obtained from each. We eschew such an approach. Not only is it the responsibility of the valuator to implement the selected method correctly, but it is also incumbent upon the valuator to justify the choice of the method selected.

INCOME-BASED VERSUS ASSET-BASED METHODS

Albeit that we only discuss four valuation methods in this book, the myriad methods that have been proffered in the academic and professional literatures fall broadly into the category of either an income-based or an asset-based approach, with one major exception that we refer to as a hybrid approach. Our discussion herein is so divided. Regarding the many valuation methods that are used, we generalize that they are simply variants of the general approaches we describe below. Of course, if there is market information on the value of a truly identical comparable business, we prefer that market value to any other value derived from a formula. As should be expected, such information rarely exists since sales or transfers of ownership in closely held businesses are confidential.

Income-based valuation methods use the business's or a comparable business's income statement as the starting point for the analysis. Similarly, asset-based methods use the business's balance sheet at the starting point. However, even when conducting an income-based analysis, the valuator should carefully study the balance sheet, and vice versa. Income statements and balance sheets describe aspects of the financial condition of the business, and hence, both should be examined. In fact, all financial information should be considered in detail.

A fundamental and extremely important assumption that underlies all business valuations is that the financial health of the business is accurately characterized by its financial statements. If the financial statements are incorrectly prepared, or if they overstate or understate the true financial picture of the going concern for some accounting reason, then it follows logically that the valuation will be imprecise.

Preparation of Financial Statements

It is generally the case that individuals trained in Generally Accepted Accounting Principles (GAAP) are involved in some way in the preparation of a business's financial statements. The involvement of a Certified Public Accountant (CPA) is not uncommon. A CPA's level of involvement with the business's financial statements can cover the spectrum from detailed to minimal. Financial statements are accordingly characterized in terms of the level of such involvement: audited, reviewed, or compiled.

An audited financial statement reflects the highest level of involvement by an independent CPA. If a statement is audited then the auditor has stated an opinion that the financial statements are presented in conformity with GAAP. The second level of involvement is called a review engagement. In such engagements, the level of investigation into the accuracy of the financial statements is generally limited to inquiry of management and analysis of selected accounts. No attempt is made to extend the scope of investigation to third-party verification of account balances. A reviewed financial statement is one for which the accountant has a reasonable basis for expressing limited assurance that there are no material modifications needed to make the financial statement conform to GAAP. An accountant's review of a financial statement is therefore insufficient to offer an opinion about the financial statement. Finally, a compiled financial statement is one for which the accountant has taken the information provided by the owner or management of the business and simply presented it in a generally accepted format without any representation as to its accuracy.

The above characterization of the level of the CPA's involvement should not be interpreted to mean that compiled financial statements are less accurate than audited financial statements, or that reviewed financial statements have only a few minor errors compared to either audited or compiled statements. On the contrary, these three American Institute of Certified Public Accountants (AICPA) categories only reflect the extent of systematic involvement of an accountant in the preparation of the financial statement and associated scrutiny of the underlying financial facts. None of the categories warrant the accuracy of the underlying numbers. Table 8.1 offers a summary of an accountant's involvement in the preparation of a financial statement.

Table 8.1
Independent Accountant Involvement in the Preparation of Financial Statements

Financial Statements	Accountant Involvement
Audited	Independent verification of accounting data by a CPA. Formation of an opinion regarding the fair presentation of the financial data in accordance with GAAP.
Reviewed	Inquiry of accounting and other personnel regarding significant operating activities and their impact on financial data. Analysis of significant accounting records without independent verification.
Compiled	Conversion of raw accounting data into financial statements. No analysis or verification of accounting data.

Pre-Tax and After-Tax Valuation Issues

Another issue relevant to any valuation is whether the valuation should be conducted on a pre-tax or an after-tax basis. The valuation profession differs with regard to this issue, and there is no definite right or wrong answer. What is important is for all parties to understand the underlying assumptions being brought to the valuation and for all parties to verify that the data used in the valuation process are consistent.

We generally conduct our valuations on a pre-tax basis. Some who frequently argue that valuations should be done on a pre-tax basis often point to the fact that courts have argued that future tax liabilities are too uncertain to be included in a valuation. In other words, while all valuators rely on assumptions regarding the future and attempt to predict future financial situations (e.g., profitability), predicting the tax rates that might be applicable to those future financial situations adds another level of judgment and an entirely new set of assumptions. Although this is true, we disagree with this position. Future tax liabilities are no more uncertain than other elements in a valuation, such as the economic conditions that will surround the business in the future. Some who frequently argue that future tax liabilities should be included do so by making the rather obvious observation that taxes are a reality of doing business.

These points aside, our justification for conducting business valuations on a pre-tax basis comes from a more pragmatic perspective. It is generally the case that the valuation is done as if there were a reasonable and fully informed buyer, when in most cases there is no buyer at all. As such, there is no a priori way to know the tax liabilities that will pertain to such a hypothetical, and it would be in our opinion speculative to assume that the potential buyer's tax structure will be the same as that of the seller. Hence, we perform our analyses on a pre-tax basis.

INCOME-BASED METHODS

Two income-based valuation methods are discussed in this section. The first is the present value of adjusted future earnings method and the second is the price-to-earnings ratio method.

Present Value of Adjusted Future Earnings

The implicit assumption underlying the present value of adjusted future earnings, or adjusted net income, is that the to-be-valued element of the business being sold is its ability to generate future earnings. The buyer is thus attempting to value a claim to a future stream of income.

A critical assumption brought to this method of analysis is how far into the future a reasonable and fully informed buyer will look when arriving at this value. That is, would a buyer look to purchasing a five-year stream of income, a ten-year stream of income, or an indefinite stream of income. If, in the opinion of the valuator, it is justifiable to impose a specific time length, then the valuation method centers around taking the present value of adjusted future earnings

($AFE), based on the income statement and other information, and using a formula analogous to that developed in Chapter 6 as equation (6.3):

$$PV = \$AFE \{[(1 + r)^n - 1]/[r(1 + r)^n]\} \qquad (8.1)$$

Or, if the valuator believes that an infinite stream of adjusted future earnings is what the buyer is purchasing, then the relevant formula is analogous to the present value formula developed in Chapter 6 in equation (6.4):

$$PV = \$AFE/r \qquad (8.2)$$

Of course, the planning horizon of the buyer may have been made explicit to the valuator, such as the case when the valuation is undertaken as advice to the buyer.

The adjusted future earnings value in either equation (8.1) or equation (8.2) should be based on a net income value that is a reasonable base from which to forecast into the future. Hence, the valuator will generally calculate a weighted average of adjusted future earnings from previous years to use for these calculations. (See Chapter 3 for a discussion of weighted averages.) Of course, just because a weighted average is generally used does not imply that a weighted average is appropriate in all situations. For example, we implied in Chapter 3 that if earnings are expected to increase in the future, then a weighted average of past values of net earnings may not be the most appropriate base to use unless of course that base is increased over time to reflect such expectations. The valuator must determine, based on the economic environment of the business, the appropriate base value for adjusted future earnings.

If equation (8.1) is used, the valuator is explicitly assuming an earnings life of n years for the business. If equation (8.2) is used, the valuator is explicitly assuming an infinite earnings life for the business. Recall from Chapter 6 that when the time period for the analysis is infinite, then the analysis is referred to as a capitalization analysis, hence, equation (8.2) is said to capitalize adjusted future earnings.

If the valuator assumes a limited earnings life for the business, then it is also reasonable to assume that after that period of time the business will still have some residual value. This residual value will have to be approximated and then incorporated into the final valuation estimate.

As discussed in previous chapters, net income is reported as a line item on an income statement. Net income is reported for each of the three to-be-valued companies in Chapter 4. However, reported net income should be adjusted, or normalized, for valuation purposes so that the being-valued company's income statement reflects how a reasonable and fully informed buyer is likely to operate the business. One of a number of important adjustments to consider is the operating expense of owner or officer compensation.

Reported net income could understate—at least in the eyes of a potential buyer—the realistic earnings of the business if the owner's compensation is viewed as having been too high. Recall that we showed in Table 7.5 that owners' compensation in Gate City Video Rental was significantly higher than the industry average, assuming of course the industry is appropriately defined. Or, reported net income could overstate the realistic earnings of the business if the owner's compensation is viewed as too low. For valuation purposes, operating expenses such as officers' compensation should be adjusted to a level that corresponds to what is reasonable for that particular business. We will illustrate this adjustment with respect to the business valuations presented in the following three chapters.

Other operating expenses that should be examined for possible adjustments are accounts receivable, charitable contributions, amortization of goodwill, depreciation, and rent. These will also be discussed in an illustrative fashion in the following chapters as relevant.

Thus, the steps to follow when using a present value of adjusted future earnings are:

- Determine if the business is perceived to have an indefinite life or a limited life of n years. If the former, then adjusted future earnings are to be capitalized; if the latter then a time period and a residual value for the business must be determined.
- Estimate an appropriate discount rate, r.
- Normalize the income statement.
- Calculate a weighted average of adjusted future earnings assuming that a weighted average of adjusted future earnings is appropriate.
- Calculate the present value of the weighted average of adjusted future earnings using either the capitalization equation (8.2) or the limited life present value equation (8.1) to which a residual value for the business must then be added, and adjust for ownership control and marketability as appropriate (discussed below).

These steps are summarized in Table 8.2, along with comments about which steps involve art and which steps involve science.

Price-to-Earnings Ratio Method

Some valuators may not view the price-to-earnings method as falling under the category of an income-based valuation method. An alternative would be to classify it under a third heading called, say, the comparable method. We do not have trouble with the latter type of classification, but we prefer to discuss the price-to-earnings ratio method as an income-based method because it is the net income or earnings of publicly traded companies that is relevant for this valuation analysis.

The present value of adjusted future earnings method or adjusted future net income method described above relies on information reported on the income statement as well as on comparable industry information for adjustment purposes. The price-to-earnings ratio method relies on the same two sources of information.

The implicit assumption underlying the price-to-earnings method is that the fair market value of the closely held business can be approximated from the market value of comparable publicly traded businesses. To implement this method, the valuator must be able to identify a set of presumed-to-be-comparable publicly traded companies and obtain sufficient information on each to verify the extent of comparability from an economic, management, and financial perspective. No publicly traded company will be precisely comparable to the closely held business being valued, so informed judgment must be exercised.

Table 8.2
Present Value of Adjusted Future Earnings Valuation Method

Steps to Follow	Comments
Determine if the business will have an indefinite life or a limited life.	This is art. Informed individuals will differ in opinion on this matter. The critical factor to consider is the economic environment that could make the goods or services produced by the business obsolete, such as technological advances. It is a time-consuming process to learn about such related industry trends, but the time is well spent to ensure an accurate valuation. It is not uncommon to see adjusted net income capitalized, without justification, because the valuator did not spend the time to investigate such trends.
Estimate an appropriate discount rate.	This is art. Informed individuals will differ in opinion about the elements of risk that characterize the business.
Normalize the income statement.	This is art. Research will need to be done on comparable companies in the industry to determine, through ratio analyses and judgment, what expenses warrant an adjustment.
Calculate a weighted average of adjusted future earnings.	This is science, assuming that a weighted average of net income is appropriate.
Calculate the present value of the weighted average of adjusted future earnings, and adjust for ownership control and marketability as appropriate.	This is both art and science. Judgment is involved regarding the appropriate ownership and marketability adjustment factors. The actual mathematical calculation is science.

As a general rule, the smaller in size and the more limited the scope of activities of the business being valued, the less likely there will be a set of publicly traded companies that are comparable, or even a single comparable publicly traded company. Publicly traded companies are for the most part large, measured in terms of revenues or assets, and they are diversified across product lines.

This diversification implies that reported revenues are from various lines of business, not all of which are relevant for comparison purposes. Also, diversification reduces the operating risk of the company, and to the extent that this reduced risk is reflected in the company's realized earnings and in the publicly reported price, the comparison may be less than accurate. Most small closely held companies are not diversified, and this characteristic alone makes financial comparisons difficult.

There are many sources for information on publicly traded companies including information provided by Value Line and Standard and Poor. Internet access to traded securities research services is the more common means to acquire the needed information.

For purposes of illustration, assume that a set of four or five comparable companies can be identified. For each company in this set, the current price-to-earnings ratio can be calculated, and then an average ratio can be calculated. It is important to emphasize that the average of the current price-to-earnings ratios is relevant for this analysis if the company is being valued at the current time. If a retrospective valuation is being conducted, then the average of the price-to-earning ratio at the appropriate historical time would be the relevant datum.

For the business being valued, the ratio of adjusted future earnings (AFE or simply E) or adjusted net income (ANI) to the number of shares outstanding (S) can be determined. The number of shares outstanding is reported in the financial statements. We note this ratio for the business being valued as $(E/S)_{business}$. The average price-to-earnings ratio for one share of the comparable companies' stock we note as $(P/E)_{comparable}$.

It follows mathematically that the market-based price per share of the business being valued equals the product of the business's earnings-to-shares ratio and the price-to-earnings ratio of comparable companies, as:

$$(P/S)_{market} = (E/S)_{business} \times (P/E)_{comparable} \tag{8.3}$$

Thus, it also follows mathematically that the market-based price or value of the business being valued is the product of the business's earnings and the price-to-earnings ratio of comparable companies, as:

$$P_{market} = E_{business} \times (P/E)_{comparable} \tag{8.4}$$

Mathematically, equation (8.4) follows from equation (8.3) by multiplying both sides of equation (8.3) by S.

Publicly Traded Marketability Adjustment

P_{market} in equation (8.4) represents the market-based price or value of the closely held company being valued. Stated alternatively, P_{market} is determined on the basis of the ratio of market prices to earnings from a comparable set of companies. Market prices from publicly held companies may be a reasonable proxy for the value of a closely held company if the companies are comparable and if the market-based price is adjusted for the fact that publicly held companies are readily marketable and closely held companies are not. Thus, the price determined from equation (8.4) must be adjusted to take into account that the closely held company is less marketable than the publicly held companies from which P_{market} was derived.

There are sources of information that a valuator can refer to for guidance on the appropriate publicly traded marketability discount—discount for lack of marketability would be a more accurate phrase although not the one that the profession uses—but the relevance of these sources for a particular valuation is questionable.

Published research on the application of marketability discounts when valuing a business on the basis of information from publicly traded companies follows two lines. One line of research is based on reviews of court cases and the marketability discount that the court has allowed. The conclusions from this line of research are interesting, but not generally applicable to a particular business valuation. First, there is selectivity bias in the sense that only those valuations that are litigated and appealed are available for such study. Second, the court's decision reflects the opinion of a judge or small group of judges, as swayed by the rhetoric of attorneys, many of whom may have less expertise in valuation than the valuator. The other line of research is based on comparisons of the price of initial public offerings of stocks to actual transaction sales, where the initial public offering is viewed as a reliable observation of fair market value in the absence of market demand. Again, there is no reason to assume that the companies involved in the initial public offerings are comparable to the particular businesses being valued.

We do not rely on either of these types of studies when determining a marketability discount to impute a valuation based on publicly traded companies. Rather, we rely on experience and informed judgment—certainly elements of art—when deciding on a marketability discount percentage. As a general rule of thumb, we use a base discount factor and we deviate from that percentage to take into account relevant aspects of the economic environment of the business. The more competitive the current and expected future environment, the higher the adjustment percentage because of fewer barriers to entry into the market. That is, a fledgling business can enter into such an industry more easily and hence the owner has less of a need to purchase a going concern as a vehicle for entry. The less competitive the current and expected future environment, the lower the marketability discount. There are even cases where a premium could be paid for a business that serves as a vehicle to enter the market if the competitive structure of the industry is driven by barriers to entry.

Our approach may be problematic for valuators to adopt if the valuation is being conducted for the purpose of litigation since our justification for our marketability discount comes from our experience rather than from others' opinions. However, it is our experience that informed courts are more receptive to valuators who are forthright when they state that the imputed publicly traded marketability discount is based on informed opinion compared to valuators who contrive some reference to what is in all likelihood others' informed opinion.

It is important to emphasize that the marketability discount discussed here applies when the closely held business is valuated on the basis of publicly traded company information. There is another appropriate use of another marketability discount when accounting for the transferability, or lack of it, of the business. We discuss the transfer marketability discount below, but note it now in Figure 8.1. The purpose of the publicly traded marketability discount is to adjust for the liquidity of ownership shares in a publicly traded company vis-à-vis that of a closely held business. From our experience in valuing closely held companies for actual sales and purchases, we have arrived at a base marketability adjustment factor of 35 percent. We deviate from the 35 percent benchmark as warranted based on our evaluation of relevant aspects of the economic environment of the business.

Figure 8.1
Marketability Discounts

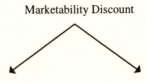

Marketability Discount

Discount the valuation value   Discount the valuation
due to potential time involved   value when based on price of
in the sale of the business   publicly traded companies

Publicly Traded Ownership Adjustment

When publicly traded companies are used as comparables, the price, P, in the price-to-earnings ratio, $(P/E)_{comparable}$, is the price of one share of traded stock. Hence, it represents the price of a minority ownership share. To value a majority position in a closely held company based on a minority ownership share from a publicly traded company requires that a premium be added to the final valuation estimate.

While there is no theoretical justification for the size of such a premium, and the academic literature related to this topic is sparse and wanting in rigor, we will simply state that our rule of thumb is to use a 15 percent premium. This percentage comes primarily from our experience in valuing companies for actual sales.

Thus, the steps to follow when using a price-to-earnings valuation method are:

- Select a sample of four or five comparable publicly traded companies and calculate the average price-to-earnings ratio for the sample, $(P/E)_{comparable}$.
- Normalize the income statement to determine $E_{business}$.

- Multiply the above two values, and then adjust the product by a publicly traded marketability discount.
- Adjust by an ownership premium.

These steps are summarized in Table 8.3.

Table 8.3
Price-to-Earnings Ratio Valuation Method

Steps to Follow	Comments
Select a sample of comparable publicly traded companies and calculate the average price-to-earnings ratio for the sample, $(P/E)_{comparable}$.	This is art. The sample selected must contain companies that are comparable not only in the sense that they operated in the same broadly defined industry, but also that their organizational and financial structure is similar. Being in the same broadly defined market need not imply that the comparable company produces the same good or service as the business being valued, rather being comparable means that the market would value the business like the comparable company if the business were publicly traded.
Normalize the income statement to determine $E_{business}$.	This is art. Research should be done on comparable companies in the industry to determine, through ratio analyses, what expenses warrant an adjustment.
Multiply the above two values, and then adjust the product by a publicly traded marketability discount factor.	This is art. Judgment is involved regarding the publicly traded marketability adjustment factor. The actual mathematical calculation is science.
Adjust by an ownership premium.	This is art. Judgment is involved in the determination of the ownership control adjustment factor.

ASSET-BASED METHODS

The pure asset-based method discussed here is the adjusted net asset method, although the capitalization of excess earnings method is partially asset based as discussed in the following section. Just as income-based valuation methods rely explicitly on the business's income statement, an asset-based valuation method relies explicitly on the balance sheet for basic financial information.

Adjusted Net Asset Method

The implicit assumption underlying the adjusted net asset method is that the market value of the business's net assets approximates a lower bound on the value of the business if the business were to be liquidated. This method is often called the adjusted liquidation method. Implementing this method is relatively straightforward. The valuator adjusts the assets on the balance sheet to their economic or market values and then subtracts from these adjusted total assets total liabilities to arrive at adjusted net assets.

It should be emphasized that assets as reflected on the balance sheet are not intended to be representative of the economic value of assets. Balance sheets prepared in accordance with GAAP reflect assets at their cost at the time of acquisition and not at their current fair market value. While circumstances will dictate what adjustments are made, the more common adjustments account for a percentage of accounts receivable not being collectable (and this percentage may be calculated based on the collection history of the business), fair market value of real property, and for the market value of goodwill.

Goodwill is a nonoperating intangible asset of some businesses. Conceptually, it represents the earning power of a business above the normal rate of return on net assets for the industry. GAAP requires that goodwill cannot be recorded as an asset unless it is acquired in an arm's-length transaction when the net assets, or a substantial portion of them, are purchased. We are of the opinion that virtually all going-concern business entities have aspects of goodwill. Customer lists, employee contacts, name recognition, accounting systems, business plans, and trained personnel are all "assets" of businesses that are not typically recorded on the balance sheet. Goodwill cannot be acquired separately. However, putting that GAAP requirement aside, not all goodwill is marketable. To the extent that recorded goodwill is not marketable, an adjustment must be made. Likewise, to the extent that the tax value of the marketable goodwill does not equal the market value, an adjustment must be made.

Thus, the steps to follow when using the adjusted net asset valuation method are:

- Adjust assets on the balance sheet to reflect fair market value.
- Determine the value of any goodwill.
- Subtract from adjusted total assets total liabilities to arrive at adjusted net assets, and then adjust for transfer marketability as appropriate.

Table 8.4 gives an annotation of the use of this method.

INCOME-BASED AND ASSET-BASED METHODS

The capitalization of excess earnings valuation method is a widely practiced method for valuing a going concern, although its historical origins clearly show that it was not intended for that use. The intended use of this method was only for the valuation of the intangible assets of a going concern.

Table 8.4
Adjusted Net Asset Valuation Method

Steps to Follow	Comments
Adjust assets on the balance sheet to reflect fair market value.	This is art. Field research will have to be done to determine the market value of certain assets, or appraised values will have to be obtained.
Determine the value of any good-will.	This is art. Judgment is involved as to the market value of such intangible assets.
Subtract from adjusted total assets total liabilities to arrive at adjusted net assets. Adjust for marketability as appropriate.	This is both art and science. Judgment is involved regarding the marketability adjustment factor. The actual mathematical calculation is science.

The origin of the concept of capitalizing excess earnings traces to the U.S. Treasury Department's "Appeals and Revenue Memorandum Number 34" (A.R.M. 34). A.R.M. 34 was issued in 1920 for the purpose of determining the amount of March 1, 1913, intangible asset value lost by breweries and other businesses connected with the distilling industry as a result of the passage of the Eighteenth Amendment to the Constitution of the United States. According to A.R.M. 34:

[Regarding] the question of providing some practical formula for determining value as of March 1, 1913, or of any other date, which might be considered as applying to intangible assets, [there is] no specific rule of guidance for determining the value of intangibles which would be applicable in all cases and under all circumstances. Where there is no established market to serve as a guide the question of value, even of tangible assets, is one largely of judgment and opinion, and the same thing is even more true of intangible assets such as good will. . . . However, there are several methods of reaching a conclusion as to the value of intangibles . . . [one of which] is to allow out of average earnings over a period of years prior to March 1, 1913, preferably not less than five years, a return of 10 per cent upon the average tangible assets for the period. The surplus earnings will then be the average amount available for return upon the value of the intangible assets, and . . . this return should be capitalized upon the basis of not more than five years' purchase—that is to say, five times the amount available as return from intangibles should be the value of the intangibles.

Aspects of A.R.M. 34 were clarified that same year by A.R.M. 68, but more importantly this "formula" approach to the fair market value of intangible assets was qualified in Revenue Ruling 68-908:

The "formula" approach [described in A.R.M. 34] should not be used if there is better evidence available from which the value of intangibles can be determined. If the assets of a going business are sold upon the basis of a rate of capitalization that can be substantiated as being realistic . . . the same rate of capitalization should be used in determining the value of the intangibles. Accordingly, the "formula" approach may be used for determining the fair market value of intangible assets of a business only if there is no better basis therefor available.

However, the Internal Revenue Service in its 1978 *IRS Appellate Conferee Valuation Training Program* denounced the frequently and often indiscriminately used formula approach in A.R.M. 34, stating:

To attempt to segregate value based on earnings as between normal income and that induced by whatever goodwill or other intangible assets the business may possess is to aspire to a higher degree of clairvoyance than has yet been demonstrated as obtainable by mere man.

In 1994, this IRS denunciation ceased to be published.

The implicit assumption underlying a capitalization of excess earnings valuation method is that a business's value can be approximated as the sum of the value of its tangible assets plus its intangible assets. Accordingly, excess earnings are defined as the difference between the weighted average of normalized net income and the return expected to be earned on a weighted average of market-valued tangible assets as discussed below. Then, so-calculated excess earnings (i.e., earnings in excess of the return expected on tangible assets) are capitalized in order to determine the estimated value of intangible assets. The value of the business is therefore the sum of the value of intangible assets and the market value of current assets. As an aside, there is no language in Revenue Ruling 68-908 to suggest that this sum is applicable to the valuation of the entire business as opposed to only the valuation of the business's intangible assets, although valuators through their practice have implicitly sanctioned this approach.

Two methods are often used to determine the expected return on the weighted average of the market value of tangible assets. When an industry wide return on assets, as found in such publications as RMA's *Annual Statement Studies*, is imputed to the market value of tangible assets, the application of the capitalization of excess earnings method is referred to as the Treasury Method. When a relatively riskless rate of return, as based on the return on low-risk financial instruments, is imputed to the market value of tangible assets, the application of the capitalization of excess earnings method is referred to as the Reasonable Rate Method or Safe Rate Method.

Thus, the steps to follow when using the capitalization of excess earnings methods are below. See Table 8.5 for an annotation of the use of this method.

- Normalize current and past net income and calculate a weighted average of normalized net income as a proxy for expected future net income.
- Determine the market value of current and past tangible assets and calculate a weighted average of the market value of tangible assets as a proxy for the expected future value of tangible assets.

- Calculate a return expected on the weighted average of the market value of tangible assets.
- Subtract the return expected on these tangible assets from the weighted average of normalized net income to determine excess earnings.
- Capitalize excess earnings.
- Add to the capitalized value of excess earnings the fair market value of current tangible assets, and adjust the sum for ownership control and marketability (as discussed below).

VALUATION ADJUSTMENTS

Regardless of which of the four valuation methods discussed above, or even other methods not discussed in this book, is used, it is generally the case that the calculated value of the business will have to be adjusted. Two adjustments referred to above are discussed here: an adjustment for ownership control and an adjustment for transfer marketability.

Minority Ownership Control

It is often the case in a business valuation that only one owner's share of a business is being valued. As a starting point, the valuator should determine the going-concern value of the entire business and then multiply that value by the percentage of the business owned by the individual. However, the analysis does not generally stop there.

The so-calculated owner's share should be further adjusted in a manner that reflects the owner's share of the business relative to the share of the other owner or owners. The purpose of this ownership control adjustment is to account for the fact that the prospective owner is purchasing not only the current earnings capabilities of the business but also the ability to influence the direction of the business and hence its expected future earnings. To the extent that the prospective owner does not have such influence, the attractiveness of owning a portion of the business is decreased; to the extent that the prospective owner does have such influence, the attractiveness of owning a portion of the business is increased. The relevant valuation question is, How much will a reasonable and fully informed buyer discount the value of the business for not having such an influence on the future direction of the business?

While there are academic and professional literatures related to ownership control adjustments, they are fragmented, and generalizations from these literatures are little more than speculation. This was the same as the situation described above with regard to the publicly traded marketability discount. From our experience in valuing closely held companies for actual sales and purchases, we have arrived at several rules of thumb that we use in our valuations. These are shown in Table 8.6 for information purposes only. We do not proffer that these are guidelines for all valuators to use; they are our guidelines based on what we have observed buyers and sellers to arrive at from the actual sale or purchase of going concerns. Again, they are rules of thumb, meaning that we frequently deviate from them depending on the particulars of the business being valuated and the role of each owner in that business.

Table 8.5
Capitalization of Excess Earnings Valuation Method

Steps to Follow	Comments
Normalize current and past net income and calculate a weighted average.	This is both art and science. Normalization is needed because the income statement must reflect the expectations of a reasonable and fully informed buyer. The calculation of a weighted average is science, assuming the weighted average of net income is appropriate.
Determine the market value of current and past tangible assets and calculate a weighted average.	This is both art and science. The market value, as opposed to the book value, of tangible assets is relevant in this calculation. Field research will have to be done to determine the market value of certain assets, or appraised values will have to be obtained, and the appropriate use of these appraisals involves judgment.
Calculate a return expected on the weighted average of the market value of tangible assets.	This is art. Judgment is involved in the definition of the industry that most closely relates to the company being valued if the Treasury Method is used; judgment is involved in the selection of an appropriate risk-free rate if the Safe Rate Method is used.
Subtract the return expected on tangible assets from the weighted average of normalized net income to arrive at excess earnings.	This is science. The phrase excess earnings refers to the fact that this business is earning an amount in excess of that which would be expected based on its marketable assets. This amount is often referred to as the intangible asset value of the business or the value of the goodwill of the business.
Determine an appropriate capitalization rate and capitalize excess earnings.	This is art. Informed individuals will differ in opinion about the elements of risk that characterize the business.
Estimate the capitalized excess earnings value of the business by adding the fair market value of current tangible assets to the capitalized value of excess earnings, and adjust for ownership control and transfer marketability.	This is both art and science. Judgment is involved in the determination of the ownership control and transfer marketability adjustment factors. The actual mathematical calculation is science.

Table 8.6
Minority Ownership Control Adjustments

Valuation Possibilities	Rules of Thumb
2 Owners	
Ownership being valued	
less than 50%	> 20%
exactly 50%	15%-25%
More than 2 Owners	
Ownership being valued	
% less than the sum of all others	>25%
% equal to sum of all others	25%

A valuator should obtain experiential information or should rely on the applicable expertise of others for insights into the quantitative aspects of ownership-control decisions as opposed to relying on the extant literature. While it is the case that some valuators will cite published studies as their so-called authority for their opinion on the adjustment percentage selected, from our perspective this is done primarily to impress a third party. In reality, experienced valuators rely exclusively on their own informed opinion, and the more confident and capable ones simply state that fact and continue on.

For liquidation purposes, no ownership adjustment, be it a minority discount or a majority premium, is required.

Transfer Marketability Adjustment

Whereas the discount rate or capitalization rate used in a fair market valuation reflects the risk of operating the going concern, a transfer adjustment rate reflects the risk and uncertainty of being able to sell the business in the real world, as opposed to being able to sell the business in a hypothetical arm's-length transaction. This adjustment likely applies to all valuations of nonpublic going concerns since none are likely to sell immediately.

Apart from the calculated fair market value of the business, there is always risk associated with the sale of a business. This risk relates to the pool of potential buyer availability within a reasonable time period as well as to the impact on business when customers realize that a sale is impending. Sale opportunities vary by geographic area, and they vary according to the current economic conditions. Whereas the being-valued business may not be cyclical in the sense that its sales and earnings increase when the economy is strong and decrease when the economy is weak, the availability of buyers may be. As we are using the term transfer marketability adjustment, it is a marketability discount that accounts for the market conditions that influence the timing of the sale of a business. This discount is distinct from our previously discussed publicly traded marketability discount that related to the use of publicly traded companies as comparables. (See again, Table 8.1.)

Based on our discussions with the owner of the business being valued as well as with owners of comparable businesses (meaning in a geographically similar sector of the economy), we have arrived at a rule of thumb for a transferability discount. Albeit a subjective adjustment, our experience has been to use a rate of 0 percent up to 15 percent. This discount applies to all valuations including liquidations.

All of the topics discussed in this chapter will be illustrated in subsequent chapters. Our illustrations are specific to Gate City Widget Company, Gate City Video Rental Company, and Gate City Orthopedic Clinic.

9

VALUATION OF GATE CITY WIDGET COMPANY

Learn, compare, collect the facts!
—Ivan Petrovich Pavlov

INTRODUCTION

This chapter presents two valuations of Gate City Widget Company. By so doing, we do not intend to contradict ourselves since we stated in Chapter 8 that there should be an a priori reason for selecting one valuation method over another. We firmly believe that, however for Gate City Widget Company we wish to illustrate two valuation methods, present value of adjusted future earnings and price-to-earnings ratio, although we would have selected the former were we valuating this business. Still, a numerical example of both is warranted for completeness of our overall explanation of valuation methods.

BACKGROUND INFORMATION

Before proceeding to illustrate the two valuation methods for Gate City Widget, we review some background information about this company. This information was originally presented in Chapter 4, but should be repeated in the event that the reader seeks to use this chapter as a self-contained reference chapter. For this reason, certain tables from Chapter 4 are reproduced here, and other tables from previous chapters are in Chapters 10 and 11.

A widget is an informal term for a gadget. Gate City Widget Company was founded in 1951 by William E. Warner, and he has been the company's only president and stockholder. The company's widgets are used by manufacturers of machine tools.

Gate City Widget Company sells its widgets throughout the southeastern United States. While there are numerous other widget companies in this region of the country, Gate City Widget has a loyal customer base and regards few of the other regional companies as viable competitors. This favorable geographic competitive position is not the primary reason behind the company's growth in sales or profitability, however. The aspects of the company's economic environment that are more relevant for business valuation purposes are not related to its domestic market but rather to the international demand for widgets by manufacturers of machine tools.

Domestic growth in machine tools between 1993 and 1997 averaged 9 percent per year, although domestic growth began to slow in 1996 and 1997. The international demand, in contrast, increased nearly 20 percent per year over this entire time period. In 1990, Gate City Widget negotiated several secure long-term contracts with major Asian companies, and these contractual relationships have accounted for the majority of the growth in its sales and the associated growth in its net income. In addition, the company initiated several labor-saving production techniques that accounted for the more rapid growth in its profits compared to its sales.

Gate City Widget Company has a promising future. While domestic demand for machine tools is forecast to decline over the next few years, this domestic decline will be more than offset by strong international growth, especially in the Asian markets. Thus, the industry should enjoy a moderate 5 to 6 percent annual rate of growth in sales through the year 2002, and the company should outperform the industry due to its international ties in the future.

Growth in sales is expected to increase in future years for at least three specific reasons. First, the company's widgets are becoming integral to the robots used in machine tool operations, and the export of machine tools is expected to increase over the next five years by between 15 and 20 percent per year. Second, U.S. machine tool builders are strategically positioned to introduce new generations of machine tools perhaps by the year 2000. When this occurs, the domestic demand for widgets will increase, and Gate City Widget's competitive position in the southeastern United States will serve it well. Third, a major concern for the metalworking and the machine tool industries is environmental standards and regulations. Environmental issues relate to the disposal of hazardous chemicals used in production. Most machine tool manufacturers have adopted new technologies to minimize the use of such fluids, and Gate City Widget's customers are some of the few machine tool companies that are at the forefront of meeting these regulations. As such, these customers are well positioned in the market to respond quickly and efficiently to increases in domestic demand.

Warner desires to have his company valued for estate planning purposes. He would like, over the next several years, to gift shares of the company to each of his three children.

The company's income statement covering the last five years is reproduced in Table 9.1 and its balance sheet for this same time period is reproduced in Table 9.2.

Table 9.1
Gate City Widget Company: Income Statement

	1993	1994	1995	1996	1997
Sales	$2,250,000	$2,520,000	$2,822,000	$3,217,000	$3,667,000
Cost of Goods Sold	1,350,000	1,512,000	1,693,000	1,930,000	2,200,000
Gross Profit	900,000	1,008,000	1,129,000	1,287,000	1,467,000
Operating Expenses:					
Officers' Compensation	175,000	189,000	204,000	220,000	238,000
Other Salaries	300,000	324,000	350,000	378,000	408,000
Payroll Taxes	40,000	44,000	47,000	51,000	55,000
Profit Sharing Plan	45,000	47,000	49,000	51,000	54,000
Office Supplies	30,000	32,000	35,000	38,000	41,000
Depreciation	25,000	30,000	35,000	40,000	45,000
Rent	125,000	125,000	125,000	125,000	125,000
Insurance	38,000	40,000	42,000	44,000	46,000
Office Supplies	25,000	26,000	27,000	28,000	29,000
Other Expenses	50,000	26,000	83,000	83,000	92,000
Total Operating Expenses	853,000	883,000	997,000	1,058,000	1,133,000
Net Income	$ 47,000	$ 125,000	$ 132,000	$ 229,000	$ 334,000

PRESENT VALUE OF ADJUSTED FUTURE EARNINGS VALUATION

After a careful and diligent review of the operating history of the company and the economic environment that the company faces and is expected to face, we have concluded that the most appropriate methodology to use to value a 100 percent interest in the company is the present value of adjusted future earnings method. While the company has a significant investment in net assets, as seen from Table 9.2 and as evidenced by its current ratio of 2.60 compared to the industry average of 1.80 as shown in Table 9.3, we have concluded that the most significant factor for determining the fair market value of the company is its ability to generate income in future years.

In addition, we have concluded that the company will continue to generate this income for an indefinite period of time. While, of course, no company has an infinite life, we have concluded that the potential life of Gate City Widget is sufficiently long that the assumption of an indefinite life is not unrealistic. This completes the first step in the present value of adjusted future earning valuation method in Table 9.4.

Table 9.2
Gate City Widget Company: Balance Sheet

	1993	1994	1995	1996	1997
Current Assets:					
Cash	$ 55,000	$ 75,000	$ 115,000	$ 205,000	$ 165,000
Accounts Receivable	325,000	373,000	425,000	568,000	753,000
Inventory	445,000	490,000	549,000	571,000	799,000
Prepaid Expenses	2,500	2,500	2,500	2,500	2,500
Total Current Assets	827,500	940,500	1,091,500	1,346,500	1,719,500
Property and Equipment:					
Manufacturing Equipment	425,000	500,000	540,000	565,000	595,000
Office Furniture and Equipment	75,000	80,000	95,000	110,000	125,000
Accumulated Depreciation	(175,000)	(205,000)	(240,000)	(280,000)	(325,000)
Total Property and Equipment	325,000	375,000	395,000	395,000	395,000
Total Assets	$1,152,500	$1,315,500	$1,486,500	$1,741,500	$2,114,500
Current Liabilities:					
Accounts Payable	$ 175,000	$ 193,000	$ 212,000	$ 233,000	$ 256,000
Bank Loan—Line of Credit	155,000	170,000	185,000	185,000	195,000
Accrued Salaries	20,000	21,000	22,000	23,000	24,000
Accrued Profit Sharing Contribution	45,000	47,000	49,000	51,000	54,000
Other Accrued Liabilities	20,000	22,000	24,000	26,000	28,000
Total Current Liabilities	415,000	453,000	492,000	518,000	557,000
Stockholders' Equity:					
Common Stock	10,000	10,000	10,000	10,000	10,000
Retained Earnings	727,500	852,500	984,500	1,213,500	1,547,500
Total Stockholders' Equity	737,500	862,500	994,500	1,223,500	1,557,500
Total Liabilities and Equity	$1,152,500	$1,315,500	$1,486,500	$1,741,500	$2,114,500

Table 9.3
Comparison of Gate City Widget Company to the Industry, 1996

Financial Ratio	Gate City Widget Company	Industry
Current ratio	2.60	1.80
Net income to sales	0.07	0.044
Return on assets	0.13	0.07
Officers' compensation to sales	0.07	0.069

Source: *Annual Statement Studies, 1997*, Robert Morris Associates, p. 220.

Table 9.4
Present Value of Adjusted Future Earnings Valuation Method

Steps to Follow	Comments
Determine if the business will have an indefinite life or a limited life.	This is art. Informed individuals will differ in opinion on this matter. The critical factor to consider is the economic environment that could make the goods or services produced by the business obsolete, such as technological advances. It is a time-consuming process to learn about such related industry trends, but the time is well spent to ensure an accurate valuation. It is not uncommon to see adjusted net income capitalized, without justification, because the valuator did not spend the time to investigate such trends.
Estimate an appropriate discount rate.	This is art. Informed individuals will differ in opinion about the elements of risk that characterize the business.
Normalize the income statement.	This is art. Research will need to be done on comparable companies in the industry to determine, through ratio analyses and judgment, what expenses warrant an adjustment.
Calculate a weighted average of adjusted future earnings.	This is science, assuming that a weighted average of net income is appropriate.
Calculate the present value of the weighted average of adjusted future earnings, and adjust for ownership control and marketability as appropriate.	This is both art and science. Judgment is involved regarding the appropriate ownership and marketability adjustments. The actual mathematical calculation is science.

Regarding the discount rate, and in this case the capitalization rate to apply in this valuation, we begin with a thirty-year Treasury bond rate of 6 percent, and then added to it percentage points that reflect aspects of risk. (The actual percentage point adjustments were arbitrarily selected for purposes of illustration.) These adjustments take into account the following aspects of risk as we see them: a declining domestic market, the possibility of export tariffs to Asian countries, few long-term contracts, and key technical people. See Table 9.5 for a more complete discussion of these constructed risk percentage point adjustments. Assume that the appropriate capitalization rate is 12 percent. This completes the second step in the present value of adjusted future earnings valuation method in Table 9.4.

After reviewing the reported results of operations of the company, we have determined that two adjustments are required to normalize the operating results. First, we determined that officers' salaries are not excessive in relationship to the industry norm. As shown in Table 9.3, officers' compensation at Gate City Widget was 7 percent of sales compared to 6.9 percent for the industry as a whole in 1996. Second, the company's income statement shows an abrupt increase in Other Expenses in 1995. After an inquiry into what was included in that category, we learned that in 1995 and 1996 the company was a defendant in a lawsuit. It incurred legal expenses of $50,000 in 1995 and $75,000 in 1996 while successfully defending the lawsuit. These expenditures are unusual and nonrecurring so they are added back to reported net income in the normalization process. The reported $92,000 of Other Expenses in 1997 is expected to continue. It represents, in part, a retainer to a marketing consulting firm.

This latter adjustment to reported net income is shown in Table 9.6. This completes the third step in the present value of adjusted future earnings valuation method in Table 9.4.

Based on the adjusted net income of Gate City Widget in Table 9.6, the weighted average of adjusted net income was calculated using a 5-4-3-2-1 weighting scheme. Given the technological changes that have characterized the production process of the company, we felt that 1997 was a more representative year than 1996. Hence, 1997 was weighted more heavily than 1996, and so on. The calculation of the weighted average is in Table 9.7. This completes the fourth step in the present value of adjusted future earnings valuation method in Table 9.3.

One could make a case that a weighted average of adjusted net income is inappropriate because the company's history is one of continuous growth and profitability. We do not disagree but for illustrative purposes we have kept with the more traditional approach of not inputting a growth factor to the weighted average.

Finally, the present value of the weighted average of adjusted net income is computed using the 12 percent capitalization rate. See Table 9.8. This value, $2,071,700 (rounded), is in our opinion the fair market value of Gate City Widget Company. Based on our extensive interviews with Mr. Warner, it is our opinion that should he decide to sell the company it would sell immediately, likely to a regional competitor. Hence, we have not discounted the value of the company by a transfer marketability factor. This completes the fifth step in the present value of adjusted future earnings valuation method in Table 9.3.

Table 9.5
Build-Up Method for Determining Discount Rates and Capitalization Rates

Steps in the Build-Up Method	Comments
Step 1 Begin with the risk-free rate of return, then add to the risk-free rate the percentage point that reflects aspects of risk.	6% based on the prevailing yield on thirty-year Treasury bonds.
Step 2 Consider adding percentage points based on the competitive environment of the business.	+ 2% because domestic markets will become more competitive as domestic demand for widgets decreases.
Step 3 Consider adding percentage points based on the regulatory environment of the business.	+ 2% based on the potential of export tariffs being imposed on Asian markets.
Step 4 Consider adding percentage points based on the cost environment of the business.	+ 0% based on domestic demand decreasing and hence input prices not increasing significantly.
Step 5 Consider adding percentage points based on the character of the customer base.	+ 1% based on favorable long-term Asian contracts, but those contracts are with only a few companies.
Step 6 Consider adding percentage points based on the nonmarketability of revenue-generating assets.	+ 1% based on the added short-term training costs should any of the key production technicians retire or leave the company.
Step 7 Consider adding percentage points based on long-term financial obligations, then add all elements together.	+ 0% based on the company's absence of long-term debt.

Total: 12%

Table 9.6
Normalization Adjustments to Gate City Widget Company's Income Statement

	1993	1994	1995	1996	1997
Net Income as Reported	$47,000	$125,000	$132,000	$229,000	$334,000
Add Back: Other Expenses	0	0	50,000	75,000	0
Adjusted Net Income	$47,000	$125,000	$182,000	$304,000	$334,000

Table 9.7
Weighted Average of Adjusted Net Income for Gate City Widget Company

Year	Adjusted Net Income	Weights	Weighted Adjusted Net Income
1993	$ 47,000	1	$ 47,000
1994	125,000	2	250,000
1995	182,000	3	546,000
1996	304,000	4	1,216,000
1997	334,000	5	1,670,000
Total		15	$3,729,000
Divide by			15
Weighted Average			$ 248,600

Table 9.8
Adjusted Future Earnings Valuation of Gate City Widget Company

Weighted Average of Adjusted Net Income	$ 248,000
Capitalization Rate	12%
Fair Market Value of Gate City Widget	$2,071,700

Mr. Warner will discuss the percentage of the company to gift to each of his three children with his accountant so as to take maximum advantage of his non-taxable gift allowance. A minority ownership discount will be applied by the accountant because each child will likely receive a small fraction of the voting shares of the company in the form of the gift.

PRICE-TO-EARNINGS RATIO VALUATION

We present this valuation approach as an alternative to the present value of adjusted future earnings valuation above. As we stated in the introduction to this chapter, we are of the opinion that a valuator should select a valuation method based on the applicability of the method to the circumstances surrounding the valuation. Our presentation of this alternative is not a contradiction to that belief or practice. Rather, Gate City Widget Company lends itself well to an illustration of how to employ a price-to-earnings valuation method, assuming that truly comparable publicly traded companies can be identified.

The steps involved in the application of the price-to-earnings valuation method are listed in Table 9.9. The first step involves the selection of a sample of comparable publicly traded widget companies. The reader would certainly question our veracity if we claimed that we conducted an exhaustive search of widget manufacturers, so assume only for purposes of illustration that a sample of hypothetical comparable companies does exist and the average price-to-earnings ratio for that sample for 1997 was 9.0.

The second step sets forth in Table 9.9 is to normalize the income statement. As discussed above with reference to Table 9.6, adjusted net income for 1997 is $334,000.

The third step involves multiplying adjustment net income by the average price-to-earnings ratio for a sample of publicly traded companies to determine the market price, per equation (8.4) derived in Chapter 8. The resulting product, as shown in Table 9.10 is $3,006,000. This computed value is then adjusted downward by a 35 percent discount rate to adjust for marketability, and this computed value is also adjusted upward by a 15 percent majority ownership premium to account for the fact that a minority ownership discount is already implicit in the publicly traded companies' prices.

As shown in Table 9.10, the price-to-earnings ratio fair market value of Gate City Widget Company is $2,404,800.

Table 9.9
Price-to-Earnings Ratio Valuation Method

Steps to Follow	Comments
Select a sample of comparable publicly traded companies and calculate the average price-to-earnings ratio for the sample, $(P/E)_{comparable}$.	This is art. The sample selected must contain companies that are comparable not only in the sense that they operated in the same broadly defined industry, but also that their organizational and financial structure is similar. Being in the same broadly defined market need not imply that the comparable company produces the same good or service as the business being valued, rather being comparable means that the market would value the business like the comparable company if the business were publicly traded.
Normalize the income statement to determine $(E)_{business}$.	This is art. Research should be done on comparable companies in the industry to determine, through ratio analyses, what expenses warrant an adjustment.
Multiply the above two values, and then adjust the product by a publicly traded marketability adjustment factor.	This is art. Judgment is involved regarding the publicly traded marketability adjustment factor. The actual mathematical calculation is science.
Adjust by an ownership premium.	This is art. Judgment is involved in the determination of the ownership control adjustment factor.

Table 9.10
Price-to-Earnings Ratio Valuation of Gate City Widget Company

Adjusted Net Income for 1997	$ 334,000
Price-to-Earnings Ratio for Comparable Companies	9.0
Valuation before Adjustments	3,006,000
Publicly Traded Marketability Discount Adjustment (35%)	(1,052,100)
Majority Ownership Premium Adjustment (15%)	450,900
Price-to-Earnings Valuation	$2,404,800

10

VALUATION OF GATE CITY VIDEO RENTAL COMPANY

Four things come not back: the spoken word; the sped arrow;
time past; the neglected opportunity.
—Omar Halif

INTRODUCTION

This chapter presents a valuation of Gate City Video Rental Company. The method selected for this valuation is the adjusted net asset valuation method, which is often referred to as the adjusted liquidation method. It may be the case that the most appropriate method to use to value a going concern is the net asset valuation method. Recall from Chapter 2 that we posited two appropriate definitions of the value of a business based on the underlying assumption of the valuation process. If the business is assumed to continue to operate, then fair market value is the appropriate definition of value; if the business is expected to cease all operations, then liquidation value is the appropriate definition of value. It is assumed in this case that Gate City Video Rental will cease operations after its sale.

BACKGROUND INFORMATION

Gate City Video Rental opened the first of its six stores in 1990. The business is owned and operated by Stanley Starling and Frederick Frost, who are equal partners.

As the company's income statement in Table 10.1 shows, revenues from movie rentals have increased slowly over the past five years, but total operating expenses have increased more rapidly. Since 1993, the net income of Gate City Video Rental has fallen, as would be expected when operating expenses grow faster than revenues—from $138,000 in 1993 to a loss of $130,000 in 1997. This decline in net income was due to an increase in operating expenses. In particular, the cost of movies increased in an amount that offset revenue increases, but in addition owners' salaries have increased at an excessive rate, in comparison to the industry. As a result, the company was not earning a positive return on its assets, although the assets of the company relative to its liabilities were not out of line for the industry. (See Table 10.2 and Table 10.3.)

Table 10.1
Gate City Video Rental: Income Statement

	1993	1994	1995	1996	1997
Movie Rentals	$2,200,000	$2,376,000	$2,566,000	$2,771,000	$2,993,000
Operating Expenses:					
Cost of Movies Rented	770,000	832,000	898,000	970,000	1,048,000
Officers' Compensation	250,000	275,000	303,000	333,000	366,000
Other Salaries	625,000	688,000	757,000	795,000	811,000
Payroll Taxes	74,000	82,000	90,000	96,000	100,000
Profit Sharing Plan	30,000	32,000	34,000	36,000	38,000
Office Supplies	30,000	32,000	35,000	38,000	41,000
Depreciation	25,000	30,000	35,000	40,000	45,000
Rent	145,000	157,000	170,000	184,000	199,000
Insurance	38,000	40,000	42,000	44,000	46,000
Office Supplies	25,000	26,000	27,000	28,000	29,000
Other Expenses	50,000	65,000	119,000	221,000	400,000
Total Operating Expenses	2,062,000	2,259,000	2,510,000	2,785,000	3,123,000
Net Income	$ 138,000	$ 117,000	$ 56,000	($ 14,000)	($130,000)

The economic environment surrounding Gate City Video Rental is characterized by competing technologies more so than by competing video rental stores. Although the company has expanded its number of stand-alone stores, it continues to face competition from other super video rental stores as well as from food stores that have begun to rent videos. More importantly, especially for valuing the company, the growth in competing technologies causes one to question the economic life of video cassette technology and hence to question the economic life of the video rental industry.

There are two important competing technologies that will have a forceful competitive impact on the video rental industry over the next five years. The first is cable television and the second is satellite dish reception. As more telephone company cable providers replace their coaxial cable with optical fibers, the quality of cable television will improve and the breadth of programming available will expand. As well, with this expansion in delivery capabilities, pay-per-view programming will rival video rentals because current releases will be available sooner and at a lower price (especially when one considers in the total price of a video rental not only the rental price at the counter but also the time needed to travel to and from the video store).

Table 10.2
Gate City Video Rental: Balance Sheet

	1993	1994	1995	1996	1997
Current Assets:					
Cash	$ 25,000	$ 65,000	$105,000	$115,000	$ 75,000
Movie Inventory	250,000	300,000	336,000	349,000	314,000
Prepaid Expenses	2,500	2,500	2,500	2,500	2,500
Total Current Assets	277,500	367,500	443,500	466,500	391,500
Property and Equipment:					
Leasehold Improvements	250,000	300,000	340,000	370,000	390,000
Office Furniture and Equipment	95,000	140,000	155,000	170,000	185,000
Accumulated Depreciation	(75,000)	(105,000)	(140,000)	(180,000)	(225,000)
Total Property and Equipment	270,000	335,000	355,000	360,000	350,000
Total Assets	$547,500	$702,500	$798,500	$826,500	$741,500
Current Liabilities:					
Accounts Payable	$200,000	$220,000	$242,000	$266,000	$293,000
Bank Loan—Line of Credit	175,000	190,000	205,000	220,000	235,000
Accrued Salaries	15,000	16,000	17,000	18,000	19,000
Accrued Profit Sharing Contribution	30,000	32,000	34,000	36,000	38,000
Other Accrued Liabilities	15,000	15,000	15,000	15,000	15,000
Total Current Liabilities	435,000	473,000	513,000	555,000	600,000
Stockholders' Equity:					
Common Stock	10,000	10,000	10,000	10,000	10,000
Retained Earnings	102,500	219,500	275,500	261,500	131,500
Total Stockholders' Equity	112,500	229,500	285,500	271,500	141,500
Total Liabilities and Equity	$547,500	$702,500	$798,500	$826,500	$741,500

Since 1995, the price of small 18-inch receiving dishes has fallen, while growth in demand has risen. Through year 2000, the projected growth in subscribers to this media is about 36 percent per year. Direct-to-home satellite broadcasting is a more recent technology than beamed satellite technology, but one that is expected to be more affordable within the next five years. As well, satellite technology will offer subscribers a wider range of viewing options than are now available via coaxial cable connections or even via optical fiber connections. Increases in subscribers to both satellite and improved cable capabilities will come at the expense of video rentals.

Table 10.3
Comparison of Gate City Video Rental to the Industry, 1996

Financial Ratio	Gate City Video Rental	Industry
Current ratio	0.84	0.9
Net income to sales	-0.005	0.065
Return on investment	not relevant	0.091
Officers' compensation to sales	0.12	0.049

Source: *Annual Statement Studies, 1997*, Robert Morris Associates, p. 940.

Starling and Frost desire to have their rental business valued because Starling wants to retire now and sell his interest in the business to Frost. Frost plans to sell, or more likely to liquidate, the business shortly thereafter.

ADJUSTED NET ASSET VALUATION

While Starling desired to sell his 50 percent interest in the company to Frost, it is our opinion, in light of the background information presented above, that the company has no going-concern value. Its value to Frost is no greater than its liquidation value.

To determine the liquidation value of Gate City Video, we followed the steps outlined in Table 10.4. First, we adjusted the assets on the balance sheet to reflect their economic value. Movie inventory, leasehold improvements, and office furniture and equipment were appraised by an independent appraiser. In addition, if the company ceases operations then prepaid expenses, which are reported on the balance sheet as a current asset, have no market value, and accrued profit sharing contributions, which are reported as a current liability, are discretionary and therefore not likely to be paid if operations cease.

These adjustments are listed in Table 10.5, which is the first step in the adjusted net asset valuation method, and the resulting fair market value of the company is $50,000. Frost should not pay Starling more than $25,000 for his 50 percent ownership in the company. No ownership control is required to this liquidation amount. We considered a transferability discount, but did not make one because Frost was immediately willing to purchase Starling's assets in the company.

Table 10.4
Adjusted Net Asset Valuation Method

Steps to Follow	Comments
Adjust assets on the balance sheet to reflect fair market value.	This is art. Field research will have to be done to determine the market value of certain assets, or appraised values will have to be obtained.
Determine the value of any goodwill.	This is art. Judgment is involved as to the market value of such intangible assets.
Subtract from adjusted total assets total liabilities to arrive at adjusted net assets. Adjust for transfer marketability as appropriate.	This is both art and science. Judgment is involved regarding the marketability adjustment factor. The actual mathematical calculation is science.

Our assumption underlying this valuation was that the company had no fair market value, meaning that it is being valued for liquidation purposes. (Recall our distinction in Chapter 2 with reference to Figure 2.2.) Fair market value is an appropriate definition of value if the business is expected to continue to operate after the sale. Other valuators might take issue with our starting point. One could argue that new management might find Gate City Video Rental a potentially attractive business and might be willing to pay above liquidation value. We do not disagree that such is a possible scenario; however, there were two important facts that swayed us toward a liquidation valuation. First, the video rental business is extremely competitive and a potential buyer inclined to enter into this business area could simply open his or her own business. Starling and Frost do not own the buildings in which they operate the business, and their leases are not automatically transferable to a new owner. Second, realizing this first point, Frost has no incentive to offer Starling more for his share of the business than Starling could receive if he were to sell it himself to a third party. And for the reasons that we just mentioned, a third party would have no incentive to pay higher than the adjusted net asset value, and would likely have an incentive to pay less than that because he or she would rationally impute an ownership control discount to the 50 percent ownership share.

Table 10.5
Adjusted Net Asset Valuation of Gate City Video Rental

	1997 Reported Book Value	1997 Adjusted Fair Market Value
Current Assets:		
Cash	$ 75,000	$ 75,000
Movie Inventory	314,000	250,000
Prepaid Expenses	2,500	0
Total Current Assets	391,500	325,000
Property and Equipment:		
Leasehold Improvements	390,000	237,000
Office Furniture and Equipment	185,000	50,000
Accumulated Depreciation	(225,000)	0
Total Property and Equipment	350,000	287,000
Total Assets	$741,500	$612,000
Current Liabilities:		
Accounts Payable	$293,000	$293,000
Bank Loan—Line of Credit	235,000	235,000
Accrued Salaries	19,000	19,000
Accrued Profit Sharing Contribution	38,000	0
Other Accrued Liabilities	15,000	15,000
Total Current Liabilities	600,000	562,000
Net Assets	$141,500	$ 50,000

11

VALUATION OF GATE CITY ORTHOPEDIC CLINIC

> The more unpopular an opinion is, the more necessary is it that the holder should
> be somewhat punctilious in his observance of conventionalities generally.
> —Samuel Butler

INTRODUCTION

In this chapter we illustrate the application of the capitalization of excess earnings valuation method to determine the fair market value of Gate City Orthopedic Clinic. Unquestionably, the most difficult aspect of the valuation of a medical practice, or any professional practice for that matter, is distinguishing between the value of the practice and the value of the physicians or professionals.
One could argue that without the physicians the medical practice has no value.
While this is true at face value, it is equally true that medical practices have dif-
fering values not only due to the presence of the physicians but also due to name
recognition, location, reputation, and so on.

BACKGROUND INFORMATION

Doctor Bruce Breslow opened Gate City Orthopedic in 1977, after previously serving on the surgical staff at Gate City Hospital. The clinic has done
very well in the past few years. Patient revenues have increased and total net
income has grown each year. The increase in patient revenue has come primarily from new patient growth rather than increases in patient charges. In fact, in
recent years revenue per patient visit has decreased. The income statement for
the clinic is in Table 11.1 and the balance sheet is in Table 11.2.

The competitive environment of the health care industry has changed significantly since 1977, and it may change even more during the next decade. It is
best described by the phrase "managed care," meaning a system of prepaid plans
for providing comprehensive coverage to members. The alleged benefit of a
managed health care is that it controls the use of health services by patients in
order to provide a cost-effective delivery of these services. The objective of

managed health care plans is to seek to partner with health care providers that are willing to provide on a contractual basis low-cost care in return for a defined patient base. Currently, over 70 percent of all physicians in the United States operate their practices under managed care.

Table 11.1
Gate City Orthopedic Clinic: Income Statement

	1993	1994	1995	1996	1997
Patient Revenues	$1,700,000	$1,836,000	$1,983,000	$2,142,000	$2,313,000
Operating Expenses:					
Physicians' Compensation	650,000	715,000	787,000	866,000	953,000
Other Salaries	325,000	358,000	394,000	433,000	476,000
Payroll Taxes	70,000	77,000	85,000	94,000	103,000
Profit Sharing Plan	85,000	89,000	93,000	98,000	103,000
Cafeteria Plan	45,000	49,000	53,000	57,000	62,000
Medical Supplies	60,000	65,000	70,000	76,000	82,000
Office Supplies	30,000	32,000	35,000	38,000	41,000
Depreciation	40,000	40,000	40,000	40,000	40,000
Rent	75,000	75,000	75,000	75,000	75,000
Malpractice Insurance	110,000	116,000	122,000	128,000	134,000
Other Insurance	45,000	47,000	49,000	51,000	54,000
Office Supplies	25,000	26,000	27,000	28,000	29,000
Bad Debts	40,000	40,000	40,000	40,000	40,000
Other Expenses	50,000	32,000	31,000	29,000	24,000
Total Operating Expenses	1,650,000	1,761,000	1,901,000	2,053,000	2,216,000
Net Income	$ 50,000	$ 75,000	$ 82,000	$ 89,000	$ 97,000

Managed health care limits the revenue potential of a given practice because payments are based on a preestablished fee schedule. As a result, there is a financial incentive for managed health care practices, especially those with one or only a few physicians, to merge or consolidate in order to achieve economies of scale in the provision of their services. In addition, hospitals are increasingly acquiring practices in order to achieve economies of scale and scope in the services that they provide, as well as controlling the referral of patients.

Breslow is the primary physician and owns 100 percent of the stock in the corporation and his salary accounts for a significant share of total physician salaries on the income statement. As noted in Table 11.3, Breslow's compensation in 1996 was $450,000, well above the industry norm. Two other physicians are on staff, each working about thirty hours per week. Breslow desires to have his practice valued in anticipation of the opportunity to sell to each of the other physicians one-third of this practice.

Table 11.2
Gate City Orthopedic Clinic: Balance Sheet

	1993	1994	1995	1996	1997
Current Assets:					
Cash	$ 25,000	$ 35,000	$ 45,000	$ 55,000	$ 65,000
Accounts Receivable	776,000	854,000	939,000	1,033,000	1,136,000
Prepaid Expenses	2,500	2,500	2,500	2,500	2,500
Total Current Assets	803,500	891,500	986,500	1,090,500	1,203,500
Property and Equipment:					
Medical Equipment	225,000	255,000	285,000	315,000	345,000
Office Furniture and Equipment	95,000	100,000	125,000	140,000	155,000
Accumulated Depreciation	(135,000)	(175,000)	(215,000)	(255,000)	(295,000)
Total Property and Equipment	185,000	190,000	195,000	200,000	205,000
Total Assets	$988,500	$1,081,500	$1,181,500	$1,290,500	$1,408,500
Current Liabilities:					
Accounts Payable	$ 55,000	$ 61,000	$ 67,000	$ 74,000	$ 81,000
Accrued Salaries	150,000	158,000	166,000	174,000	183,000
Accrued Profit Sharing Contribution	85,000	89,000	93,000	98,000	103,000
Other Accrued Liabilities	15,000	15,000	15,000	15,000	15,000
Total Current Liabilities	305,000	323,000	341,000	361,000	382,000
Stockholders' Equity:					
Common Stock	10,000	10,000	10,000	10,000	10,000
Retained Earnings	673,500	748,500	830,500	919,500	1,016,500
Total Stockholders' Equity	683,500	758,500	840,500	929,500	1,026,500
Total Liabilities and Equity	$988,500	$1,081,500	$1,181,500	$1,290,500	$1,408,500

CAPITALIZATION OF EXCESS EARNINGS VALUATION METHOD

Recall from Chapter 8 that the capitalization of excess earnings valuation method was characterized as a hybrid, meaning that it combines elements of an income-based valuation method and of an asset-based valuation method. This valuation method thus considers both the net assets owned by the clinic and the earning potential of the clinic.

Table 11.3
Comparison of Gate City Orthopedic Clinic to the Industry, 1996

Financial Element	Gate City Orthopedic Clinic	Industry
Compensation per physician	$450,000	$310,475

Source: Physician Compensation and Production Survey: 1997 Report Based on 1996 Data, Medical Group Management Association, p. 26.

As Table 11.4 indicates, the first and second steps in the method are to normalize net income and net assets, and this is done in Table 11.5 and Table 11.6 without a detailed explanation since it is the general method that we seek to illustrate. The normalization adjustments are to adjust physicians' salaries to the industry norm, and to adjust net assets for noncollectable accounts receivable. Weighted average of both adjusted net income and adjusted net assets are computed in Table 11.7 and Table 11.8, respectively.

This third step in Table 11.4 is to calculated the return expected on the weighted average of the market value of tangible net assets. Our analysis illustrates the Safe Rate Method, a risk-free rate of 6.0 percent is used, as was previously used in the valuation of Gate City Widget Company in Table 9.5. Excess earnings over the safe rate earned on tangible net assets are $175,570, as shown in Table 11.9.

We have determined that the appropriate capitalization rate to apply to these excess earnings is 29 percent. Above the risk-free rate of 6 percent we have added 23 percentage points to reflect, primarily, the regulatory environment of the business as associated with managed health care and the potential that Dr. Breslow's revenue-generating capacity is not directly transferable to the two purchasing partners. Thus, as shown in Table 11.9, the capitalized value of excess earnings, or as we have labeled it in the table, the intangible value (and many valuators will call this the goodwill of the clinic), of the clinic is $605,414. The sum of the clinic's current tangible and intangible assets is thus, $1,461,914.

We have applied an ownership adjustment discount to this resulting value. While 100 percent of the clinic is being valued, the known buyers are the two other physicians currently in the practice. Each intends to be a 33 percent owner, and hence each will have equal ownership control of the business. We have used a 25 percent discount to account for this fact. (See Table 8.6.) We have not considered a transferability discount because the purpose of the valuation was for a know sale of the clinic to the other physicians. In our opinion, the fair market value of Gate City Orthopedic Clinic for this particular valuation is $1,461,914, and thus the sales price to each of the other parties is one-third of that amount less 25 percent for a minority ownership discount adjustment, or $361,824. (See Table 11.9.)

Table 11.4
Capitalization of Excess Earnings Valuation Method

Steps to Follow	Comments
Normalize current and past net income and calculate a weighted average.	This is both art and science. Normalization is needed because the income statement must reflect the expectations of a reasonable and fully informed buyer. The calculation of a weighted average is science, assuming the weighted average of net income is appropriate.
Determine the market value of current and past tangible assets and calculate a weighted average.	This is both art and science. The market value, as opposed to the book value, of tangible assets is relevant in this calculation. Field research will have to be done to determine the market value of certain assets, or appraised values will have to be obtained, and the appropriate use of these appraisals involves judgment.
Calculate a return expected on the weighted average of the market value of tangible assets.	This is art. Judgment is involved in the definition of the industry that most closely relates to the company being valued if the Treasury Method is used; judgment is involved in the selection of an appropriate risk-free rate if the Safe Rate Method is used.
Subtract the return expected on tangible assets from the weighted average of normalized net income to arrive at excess earnings.	This is science. The phrase excess earnings refers to the fact that this business is earning an amount in excess of that which would be expected based on its marketable assets. This amount is often referred to as the intangible asset value of the business or the value of the goodwill of the business.
Determine an appropriate capitalization rate and capitalize excess earnings.	This is art. Informed individuals will differ in opinion about the elements of risk that characterize the business.
Estimate the capitalized excess earnings value of the business by adding the fair market value of current tangible assets to the capitalized value of excess earnings, and adjust for ownership control and transfer marketability.	This is both art and science. Judgment is involved in the determination of the ownership control and transfer marketability adjustment factors. The actual mathematical calculation is science.

Table 11.5
Normalization Adjustments to Gate City Orthopedic Clinic's Income Statement

	1993	1994	1995	1996	1997
Net Income as Reported	$ 50,000	$ 75,000	$ 82,000	$ 89,000	$ 97,000
Add Back: Physicians' Compensation	650,000	715,000	787,000	866,000	953,000
Less: "Normal" Physicians' Compensation (rounded)	(575,000)	(621,000)	(671,000)	(725,000)	(783,000)
Adjusted Net Income	$125,000	$169,000	$198,000	$230,000	$267,000

Table 11.6
Normalization Adjustments to Gate City Orthopedic Clinic's Balance Sheet

	1993	1994	1995	1996	1997
Net Assets as Reported	$683,500	$758,500	$840,500	$929,500	$1,026,500
Less: 15% Allowance for Noncollectable Accounts Receivable (rounded)	(116,000)	(128,000)	(141,000)	(155,000)	(170,000)
Adjusted Net Assets	$567,500	$630,500	$699,500	$774,500	$ 856,500

Table 11.7
Weighted Average of Adjusted Net Income for Gate City Orthopedic Clinic

Year	Adjusted Net Income	Weights	Weighted Adjusted Net Income
1993	$125,000	1	$ 125,000
1994	169,000	2	338,000
1995	198,000	3	594,000
1996	230,000	4	920,000
1997	267,000	5	1,335,000
Total		15	$3,312,000
Divide by			15
Weighted Average			$ 220,800

Table 11.8
Weighted Average of Adjusted Net Assets for Gate City Orthopedic Clinic

Year	Adjusted Net Assets	Weights	Weighted Adjusted Net Assets
1993	$567,500	1	$ 567,500
1994	630,500	2	1,261,000
1995	699,500	3	2,098,500
1996	774,500	4	3,098,000
1997	856,500	5	4,282,500
Total		15	$11,307,500
Divide by			15
Weighted Average			$ 753,833

Table 11.9
Capitalization of Excess Earnings Valuation of Gate City Orthopedic Clinic

Weighted Average of Net Income	$ 220,800
Adjusted Net Tangible Assets	753,833
Safe Rate of Return	6.0%
Safe Return on Net Tangible Assets	45,230
Excess Earnings over the Safe Rate Return	175,570
Capitalization Rate	29%
Value of Intangible Assets	605,414
1997 Adjusted Net Assets	856,500
Valuation before Adjustments	1,461,914
% being valued	33%
Proportional Value of the Clinic	482,432
Minority Ownership Discount Adjustment (25%)	(120,608)
Capitalization of Excess Earnings Valuation of 33% of the Clinic	$ 361,824

12

CONCLUSION

Omit needless words.
—William Strunk, Jr.

Eschew Obfuscation
—Anonymous

We conclude this business valuation primer with a summary list of the critical points that we have developed in the previous chapters. We present them in a logical order in an effort to reinforce the fact that there are elements of both art and science in the conduct of business valuations.

- Business valuations are conducted for myriad reasons.
- The number of business valuations conducted each year has likely been increasing. Business valuation is rapidly becoming a vocation unto itself.
- The preferred method for calculating the value of a business is to rely on truly identical comparable business sales; however, rarely does that information exist.
- The choice of a valuation method depends on the definition of value that is appropriate to the valuation; fair market value versus liquidation value.
- The financial data that describe a company should be understood not only in terms of the accounting conventions used in its preparation but also in terms of the economic environment of the business.
- Fundamental to the determination of a discount rate or capitalization rate is an understanding of the elements of risk that characterize the business. The most contemplated aspect of a business valuation is the quantification of the risk of the business.
- There are many dimensions of comparability as related to business valuations. These dimensions are broader than a simple industry classification.
- Business valuation methods fall broadly into two categories, income-based methods and asset-based methods. No one valuation method is applicable to all valuations.
- While all valuation methods have sequential steps to follow in their implementation, each step involves some aspect of informed judgment.

Given these summary points, we emphasize again that business valuations involve both art and science. We have yet to see a business valuation that does not blend the two. Recall that no two valuations—meaning the situations and the attendant methodological considerations about the valuation—are ever the same. As such, each valuation should be approached with an open mind toward the situations that define the valuation and thus make it unique. Then, having done this, judgment based on experience will serve the valuator well.

GLOSSARY

Accounting: An information system that accumulates, processes, and communicates information, primarily financial in nature, about a specific economic entity.

Accounting Equation: Expresses the relationship between assets, liabilities, and owners' equity as: Assets - Liabilities = Owners' Equity.

Accounting Profit: Refers to the amount remaining after all costs have been deducted from revenues.

Accrual-Basis Accounting: A type of accounting concerned with the economic consequences of events and transactions rather than only with the cash receipts and cash payments. *See also* **Cash-Basis Accounting**

Acquisition: *See* **Merger**

Activity Ratio: An indicator of the efficiency with which a company used its economic resources. *See also* **Liquidity Ratio**

Alternative Cost: *See* **Opportunity Cost**

Annuity: A series of equal cash payments occurring at equal intervals over a period of time. If the first payment occurs at the end of the first period, the annuity is called an ordinary annuity; if it occurs at the beginning of the first period, it is called an annuity due.

Appreciation: An increase in value.

Assets: Probable future economic benefits obtained or controlled by a particular entity as a result of past transactions or events.

Assumptions: The foundation of an analysis is based on stating premises that are believed to be true.

Audited Financial Statement: A financial statement accompanied by a CPA's opinion regarding the fair presentation of the financial data in accordance with GAAP.

Average: A measure of central tendency. Three common measures are the mean, median, and mode. *See also* **Mean; Median; Mode**

Balance Sheet: A report that shows the financial position of a business at a particular point in time. Assets are shown in the order of their liquidity, and liabilities are shown in the order of their maturity date.

Bank: A company authorized by federal òr state charter to perform various financial activities including: deposit functions, payment functions, credit functions, investment functions, and service functions.

Bankruptcy: A judicial procedure used to recognize conflicting interests between a debtor and a creditor.

Best Fit: Given an estimating criterion, there is one regression line that fits a data set better than any other line. *See also* **Least-Squares Estimation; Regression Analysis**

Beta Coefficient: A number, based on theoretical calculations, that reflects how a particular publicly traded stock has historically moved compared to the stock market as a whole.

Bill: An instrument of debt that is issued for a short period of time, generally less than one year. *See also* **Bond**

Bond: A written, unconditional promise to pay a specific sum at a specific future date, along with interest, at a fixed rate and at fixed dates. *See also* **Bill**

Book Value: A term that refers to the carrying value of an item on the financial statement of a company. Book value, unlike market value, reflects the accounting principles and methods used in preparing the financial statements of the company.

Business Cycle: A sequence of expansions and contractions in various economic processes that show up as major fluctuations in overall economic activity.

Buy/Sell Agreement: A contractual agreement that not only restricts the transfer of ownership of a business but also establishes methodologies for valuing those ownership assets.

Capital: Refers in economics to the physical inputs used in production such as the plant and equipment. In a narrow sense, capital is sometimes used to refer to money. In accounting, capital is the residual interest in the assets of an entity that remains after deducting liabilities. Hence, capital is ownership interest.

Capital Asset Pricing Model: One method for estimating the cost of equity capital for an issuing company. The model treats a stock as one potential element of an investor's portfolio, and as such the stock is evaluated in terms of its influence on the entire portfolio in terms of its return and risk. It is assumed that the cost of equity capital equals the sum of the return on a risk-free investment and a premium that reflects the risk of the equity.

Capital Budgeting: The process of planning for a capital expenditure.

Capital Gain/Loss: The profit/loss to an investor, either an individual or a company, from an investment asset.

Capital Structure Ratio: Ratio that reflects the long-term solvency of the business.

Capitalization: The process of determining the present value of an infinitely lived asset.

Capitalization Factor: The reciprocal of the capitalization rate.

Capitalization Rate: Sometimes referred to as the cap rate, it is the discount rate used in the present value calculation of an infinitely lived asset.

Cash: Money.

Cash-Basis Accounting: Recognizes only transactions involving actual cash receipts and disbursements occurring in a given period. *See also* **Accrual-Basis Accounting**

Cash Flow: Refers to the total cash receipts from sales, less the actual cash expenditures required to obtain those sales.

Cash Management: Cash is an important working asset of a company. The objectives of cash management are to keep the amount of a company's cash available within prescribed limits, to keep the cost of borrowing cash to a minimum, and to invest cash at the maximum return acceptable to the company.

Central Tendency: Measures of central tendency are also called averages. *See also* **Mean; Median; Mode**

Closely Held Business: The ownership in a closely held business or company is held by one or more individuals. There is no publicly traded stock.

Coincident Economic Indicator: *See* **Economic Indicator**

Competition: A general term referring to the process through which sellers rival each other for some goal such as sales or market shares.

Compiled Financial Statement: The conversion of raw accounting data into financial statements. No analysis or verification of accounting data has been done.

Compound Interest: Refers to interest being earned on interest previously earned.

Comptroller: The chief accounting executive in a company. Often a treasurer assumes this responsibility.

Consumer Price Index: (CPI) A price index that compares the prices of goods and services in the current year to those in a base year.

Corporation: An entity created by law, capable of owning assets, incurring liabilities, and engaging in specified activities.

Cost of Capital: The average of the cost of each type of debt and equity capital issued by a company. The cost of capital also refers to the discount rate that equates the expected present value of future cash flows to common shareholders with the market value of the common stock at a specific time.

Credit: Refers to a legal obligation to make repayment at a later date for goods, services, or money obtained through the extension of credit.

Current Assets: Those economic resources of a business entity that are held in the form of cash and those that are reasonably expended to be sold, consumed, or converted into cash during the normal operating cycle of the company or within one year.

Current Liabilities: The obligations that must be discharged with the normal operation cycle of a company or within one year, whichever is longer.

Current Value: *See* **Present Value**

Curve Fitting: The use of statistical methods to represent functionally a set of data. *See also* **Regression Analysis**

Data: Numerical representations of business and economic activities.

Debt: In general refers to something owed. Corporate debt refers to the liabilities of a company. Relatedly, the term issuing debt refers to companies selling liabilities such as bonds.

Debt-Equity Ratio: A measure of a company's ability to repay its long-term obligations. It equals total debt divided by total stockholders' equity.

Default Risk: The probability that a borrower will be unable to repay a debt.

Deficit: At the company level, an excess of dividends and losses over earnings that results in a negative retained earnings balance.

Demand Curve: A graphical illustration of the decreasing relationship between price and quantity demand. Price is shown on the vertical axis and quantity demanded is on the horizontal axis.

Depreciation: The accounting process of allocating in a systematic and rational manner the cost or the other basic value of a tangible, long-lived asset net of salvage value over the estimated useful life of the asset.

Discount Rate: The rate used in present value calculations. It represents the market rate of interest for alternative investments of equal risk.

Discounted Cash Flow: A method for determining the fair market value of a going concern. The value of the going concern equals the discounted value of expected future cash flows.

Discounting: *See* **Present Value**

Diseconomies of Scale: Inefficiencies (diseconomies) associated with size (scale) per se of a business. As businesses become too large, inefficiencies in all aspects of operation can occur. *See also* **Economies of Scale**

Dividend: A distribution of cash, other assets, liabilities, or a company's own stock to shareholders in proportion to the number of shares of stock they own.

Dividend Payout Ratio: The ratio of dividends declared for the fiscal year to the net income of the company for that year.

Duopoly: A market structure characterized by two sellers.

Earnings: The net income of a company. Earnings of a company can either be retained by the company or distributed to stockholders.

Earnings Per Share: The ratio of the net income of the company divided by the number of shares of outstanding stock. It is a profitability ratio.

Economic Indicator: A series of data whose movements correspond to changes in the level of economic activity. Economic indicators fall into three broad categories: leading (move ahead of the economy) economic indicators; co-incident (move with the economy) economic indicators; and lagging (move after the economy) economic indicators.

Economics: The study of choices by members of a society. Members include government officials, producers of goods and services, and consumers of goods and services.

Economies of Scale: Production efficiencies (economies) associated with the size of scale of a business' operations. *See also* **Diseconomies of Scale**

Economies of Scope: A cost advantage may be gained by a company when it produces several different products using similar production processes. The ability to gain this advantage is said to be due to economies (efficiencies) of scope (diversification).

Entry and Exit Barriers: Barriers to entry into a market or exit from a market are examples of market imperfections. These barriers do not distort the economic efficiency associated with competitive markets; they imply, however, that competitive forces will not act instantaneously.

Equilibrium: A market is said to be in equilibrium where there is no tendency for a price or quantity to change.

Equilibrium Price: The price that corresponds to the equilibrium quantity, which is where supply equals demand. *See also* **Equilibrium**

Equilibrium Quantity: The equilibrium quantity is the quantity associated with supply equal to demand. *See also* **Equilibrium**

Equity: It is common for a corporation to acquire funds, or capital, in one of two ways: by issuing stock or by selling bonds. Equity refers to the stock issued by a corporation, or more broadly to the ownership per se.

Exchange Rate: The price at which one country's currency can be exchanged for another country's currency.

Exit: A company is said to exit from a market when it voluntarily or involuntarily leaves the market.

Expectations: Refers to expected future values of economic variables.

Factor Markets: There are markets for all factors of production. These markets work according to the laws of supply and demand. Equilibrium in factor markets determines the market price of the factors.

Factor Substitution: Factors of production are substitutable in many production processes. Companies will substitute one factor for another in response to changes in the relative prices of the factors.

Factors of Production: Generally, a company's factors of production are capital, labor, and land. In theory each factor makes its own contribution, but many factors work interdependently.

Fair Market Value: Refers to the price at which property would change hands between a willing and informed buyer and a willing and informed seller, neither under compulsion to buy or sell.

Fiduciary: A person who holds something in trust for another.

Financial Markets: Markets that bring together borrowers and lenders.

Fixed Asset: A company's long-lived nonfinancial capital assets, like plant and equipment.

Forecasting: A statistical technique used to make judgments about future events based on an analysis of past events and other factors that might affect those future events. *See also* **Trend Line**

Frictional Unemployment: The state of individuals who at any given time are literally between jobs.

Future Value: The result of interest being applied to principal over time. *See also* **Present Value**

Goods and Services: The phrase used to represent all output from production processes.

Goodwill: A nonoperating intangible asset of some businesses. Conceptually, it represents the earnings power of a business above the nominal rate of return on net assets for the appropriate industry.

Gross Domestic Product: (GDP) The official measure of the nation's production of output rather than Gross National Product (GNP). GDP includes the value of goods and services produced within the geographic boundaries of a country.

Gross Profit: *See* **Profit**

Hard Core Unemployment: The state of those individuals who are having the most difficult time finding employment possibly due to physical limitations, age, mental conditions, or a general attitude against working.

Hidden Unemployment: The state of individuals who during a recession have become discouraged and quit looking for employment. They would like to work but are not counted in the unemployment statistics because they have quit looking for employment.

Historical Cost: In terms of capital this is the original, or book cost, of the plant and equipment of a business.

Implicit Cost: *See* **Opportunity Cost**

Income: Refers to the amount that results from the deduction of costs of goods sold and other expenses and losses from revenue. On an income statement, the calculation is: Revenues - Expenses + Gains - Losses = Net Income.

Income Statement: Part of a company's overall financial statement that presents the results of operations for an accounting period.

Industry: A collection of all companies producing closely substitutable products. Because there is no operational definition of what closely substitutable products are, the U.S. government, like governments in other industrialized nations, has established standard industrial classification (SIC) codes for reporting of industrial data.

Inflation: A persistent increase in the price level in general for specific goods and services.

Innovation: An invention put into use. Use is the key term when distinguishing an innovation from an invention. *See also* **Invention**

Intercept: The point on either the vertical or horizontal axis that is intersected by a function.

Interest: The cost of using money over time. From the perspective of a lender, interest is the excess money that is received over the amount that was loaned. The amount of interest charged reflects the time value of money due to inflation and the risk associated with the loan.

Invention: The creation of something new. *See also* **Innovation**

Inventory: Reserve final goods and intermediate goods held to meet unexpected increases in the demand of its products.

Journal Entry: A chronological record of a company's events and transactions. Journal entries generally follow accepted accounting practices.

Junk Bond: Originally used to denote the outstanding bonds issued by a company suffering current financial troubles. The term is also used to refer to speculative grade debt, regardless of the financial condition of the issuing company.

Labor: Refers to services provided by workers of all types and skills.

Labor Force: All persons sixteen years and older who are either employed or are actively seeking employment.

Labor Productivity: The amount of output produced by a worker. It is measured generally as the ratio of output per unit of labor when labor units are in number of workers or in number of person-hours.

Lagging Economic Indicator: *See* **Economic Indicator**

Law of Demand: The quantity of a product that consumers are willing to purchase. Economists believe that there is a predictable negative relationship between price and quantity demanded, all other things remaining constant. This relationship is called the Law of Demand.

Law of Supply: The quantity of a product that producers are willing to produce. Economists believe that there is a predictable positive relationship between price and quantity supplied, all other things remaining constant. This relationship is called the Law of Supply or the Theory of Supply.

Leading Economic Indicator: *See* **Economic Indicator**

Least-Squares Estimation: The criterion used in regression analysis to define the best straight line to fit a set of data. The line for which the sum of squared deviations of actual data from fitted data is a minimum is the least-squares line. *See also* **Regression Analysis**

Leverage: Used to explain a business's ability to use fixed assets or funds to magnify the returns to its owners.

Licensing: An operations requirement by the state to ensure that certain businesses and professional practices maintain acceptable levels of services.

Linear Regression: *See* **Regression Analysis**

Liquid Asset: *See* **Liquidity**

Liquidation Value: The monetary value collectable when the business's operations cease and net assets are sold.

Liquidity: Describes the amount of time required to convert an asset into cash or to pay a liability.

Liquidity Ratio: Describes the company's liquidity or the ability of the business to meet its current financial obligations. Such ratios generally relate working capital or current assets to liabilities.

Loan: Money advanced from a lender to a borrower in return for the promise to repay the money at a specified future date.

Long-Term Capital: The long-term financial debt of a company.

Management: The process by which human efforts are coordinated and combined with other resources to accomplish organizational goals and objectives.

Marginal Analysis: The single most pervasive concept in economics. Marginal refers to additional, or incremental. Decision making is described in terms of marginal benefits and marginal costs. The marginal rule applies when economic decisions are made when marginal benefits are greater than marginal costs.

Market: A conceptual term in economics that refers to the economic exchange of a particular resource or product. A market is not necessarily a physical place. Rather, the concept of a market refers to the entire network of formal and informal mechanisms for exchange.

Market Analysis: The analysis that an investor will undertake in order to understand a market before investing in a company that operates in that market.

Market Equilibrium: *See* **Equilibrium**

Marketability Adjustment: An adjustment made to the calculated value of a closely held business to account for the use of publicly traded company earnings information in the valuation of the closely held business and/or to account for transfer costs in selling the business.

Mean: A measure of central tendency calculated as the sum of all observations in a data set divided by the number of observations in the data set.

Median: A measure of central tendency in a data set above and below which 50 percent of the observations lie.

Merger: The combining of one company with another for the sake of profit.

Minimum Wage: The legally required minimum to be paid to a worker.

Mode: A measure of central tendency. Within a set of data the mode is the most frequently observed datum.

Money: An accepted medium of exchange in an economy.

Monopoly: A market structure in which there is only one supplier of a product. There are significant barriers to entry into such an industry. The price prevailing under a monopoly market structure will be higher than the price that would prevail under a more competitive market structure.

Net Book Value: *See* **Book Value**

Net Income: *See* **Earnings**

Net Profit: Total profit less depreciation costs and sometimes less tax obligations. *See also* **Profit**

Nominal Value: Refers to monetary value. *See also* **Real Value**

Normalize: To recast the operating activity of the business so as to reflect how a potential buyer might operate the business.

Oligopoly: A market structure characterized by a few (more than two) sellers.

Opportunity Cost: Represents the value of any foregone (lost) activity. This concept is fundamental in economics because it underscores the fact that all resources have alternative uses.

Option: A marketable security that provides for the future exchange of cash and common shares contingent upon the option owner's choice.

Ordinary Least Squares: *See* **Least-Squares Analysis**

Ownership Control Adjustment: An adjustment made to the calculated value of a closely held business to account for the degree of ownership control of the portion of the business being valued.

Partnership: An association of two or more individuals who act as co-owners to carry on a business for profit.

Patent: An exclusive right granted to an individual or company by the government to use a particular process or to make or sell a specific product for a predetermined period of time.

Perfect Competition: The process through which companies adjust to changes in the activities of other companies in the market. Perfect competition is a conceptual form of market structure where all companies produce a homogeneous product and have perfect information of all market events.

Portfolio: Generally refers to an individual's or company's collection of investment assets.

Present Value: The principal that must be invested at time zero to produce a known future value.

Price Index: A comparison of the prices of goods and services in the current year to those in a base year. *See also* **Consumer Price Index**

Prime Rate: The interest rate that banks charge to the best and safest customers.

Principal: The amount of money paid to the holder of a bond, or similar financial obligation, when it matures.

Probability: A number that reflects the chances that an event will occur.

Profit: The financial reward for taking risk. In accounting it refers to the amount remaining after the cost of goods sold has been deducted from revenues.

Profitability Ratio: A financial ratio that reflects the extent to which the business is operating in a profitable manner.

Public Company: A company that is owned by outside stockholders, as opposed to a closely held company.

Publicly Traded Company: A public company that offers its ownership shares in an organized public market, or stock exchange.

Publicly Traded Marketability Discount: *See* **Marketability Adjustment**

Quota: A limit imposed by the government upon producers in selected industries to control the supply of identified products that can be imported into a country.

Range: A set of data that is the absolute difference between the highest and lowest value in the set.

Ratio: An expression of a mathematical relationship between one quantity and another.

Real Value: An inflation adjusted value. *See also* **Nominal Value**

Regression Analysis: In an equation where it is hypothesized that the variable Y is functionally related to a set of independent variables. In the bivariate (two variable case), there is only one independent variable. If the functional form of the hypothesized relationship is linear, then the regression analysis is said to be a linear regression analysis. The associated analysis used to estimate the hypothesized relationship is called regression analysis, and it is based on least-squares analysis. *See also* **Least-Squares Estimation**

Retained Earnings: The earnings of a company that have not been distributed in the form of dividends.

Revenue Ruling: Published opinions of the Internal Revenue Service regarding various tax issues.

Reviewed Financial Statement: A statement that reflects that an accountant has analyzed significant accounting records in preparing it but has not done an independent verification.

Risk: The probability that the actual return on an investment will differ from its expected return. From a statistical point of view, risk can be measured in probability terms. *See also* **Uncertainty**

Risk Premium: The amount used to increase the discount rate used in a present value analysis to account for the possibility that the future income of investment return might not be realized.

Sales: Major business transactions involving the delivery of goods, merchandise, services, properties, and rights in exchange for cash or money equivalents.

Salvage Value: The value of the capital at the end of its productive life, in terms of depreciation.

Sampling: The process used by statisticians for selecting a sample of data from the population.

Scrap Value: *See* **Salvage Value**

Services: Activities, as opposed to tangible goods, that are exchanged in a market.

Speculation: The buying or selling of assets in anticipation of making a profit from reselling or rebuying them.

Standard Industrial Classification: (SIC) *See* **Industry**

Sunk Cost: The costs previously invested in a product that are lost, or are considered nonrecoverable when a business abandons the production of a particular product.

Tax Incidence: Refers to the individual(s) who actually bear the burden of the tax.

Technology: Refers, in a narrow sense, to specific physical tools, but in a broader sense it describes how such tools affect the production process.

Term Structure of Interest Rates: The relationship between the yield on securities and their time to maturity. Generally, the longer the time to maturity the higher the interest rate paid on the security.

Theory of Supply: *See* **Law of Supply**

Transfer Marketability Discount: *See* **Marketability Adjustment**

Trend Line: A linear representation of historical data from which a forecast of future data can be made by linear extrapolation.

Trust: A fiduciary relationship under which property is held by one person, a trustee, for the benefit of another, the beneficiary.

Uncertainty: A situation in which a decision maker does not have information about the outcomes of an action and, unlike with risk, no estimate can be made about the probabilities associated with the alternative outcomes. *See also* **Risk**

Unemployment: The state of individuals that are in the labor force and are actively seeking employment.

Usury: Refers to the charging of interest on borrowed money.

Valuation: The application of methods to determine the value of a going concern or of its assets.

Voluntary Unemployment: The state of an individual who is voluntarily unemployed if that individual quits a job and continues to remain in the labor force and search for new employment.

Wages: The prices paid to workers.

Weighted Average: A method of averaging data where particular data are weighted or treated differently in the mathematical calculation than other data.

Yield Curve: *See* **Term Structure of Interest Rates**

REFERENCES

Annual Statement Studies, 1997. Philadelphia: Robert Morris Associates, 1997.

Badger, Ralph. *Valuation of Industrial Securities.* New York: McGraw-Hill, 1925.

Dewing, Arthur S. *The Financial Policy of Corporations.* New York: Ronald Press, 1953.

Physician Compensation and Production Survey: 1997 Report Based on 1996 Data. Englewood, CO: Medical Group Management Association, 1997.

Schlit, James. "A Rational Approach to Capitalization Rates for Discounting the Future Income Stream of a Closely Held Company." *The Financial Planner,* January 1982.

Stocks, Bonds, Bills, and Inflation. Chicago: R. G. Ibbotson Associates, 1997.

U.S. Department of Commerce. *Statistical Abstract of the United States, 1998.* Washington, DC: U.S. Government Printing Office, 1998.

U.S. Department of Commerce. *U.S. Industry & Trade Outlook, 1998.* New York: McGraw-Hill, 1998.

U.S. Internal Revenue Service. *IRS Appellate Conferee Valuation Training Program.* Chicago: Commerce Cleaning House, 1978.

U.S. Internal Revenue Service Revenue Ruling 59-60.

U.S. Internal Revenue Service Revenue Ruling 65-192.

U.S. Internal Revenue Service Revenue Ruling 65-193.

U.S. Internal Revenue Service Revenue Ruling 68-609.

U.S. Internal Revenue Service Revenue Ruling 77-287.

U.S. Internal Revenue Service Revenue Ruling 80-213.

U.S. Internal Revenue Service Revenue Ruling 83-120.

U.S. Treasury, "Appeals and Revenue Memorandum Number 34."

Wall Street Journal, various issues.

INDEX

About the Authors

ALBERT N. LINK is Professor of Economics at the University of North Carolina at Greensboro. He is the author of numerous academic and professional books, including *Evaluating Economic Damages* (Quorum, 1992) and *Evaluating Public Sector Research and Development* (Praeger, 1996).

MICHAEL B. BOGER is a partner in the accounting firm of Breslow Starling Frost Warner & Boger, PLLC. In 1995 he became a Certified Valuation Analyst.